T0048989

PRAISE FOR STRESS LESS

"Written by a leading expert on emotional wellness in teens, *Stress Less* shares tried and true methods for coping with stress and reducing its impact on your life. This book is packed with practical, step-by-step tips for living well in the face of stress. I highly recommend it!"

Martin M. Antony, PhD
Professor of Psychology, Toronto Metropolitan University
Author of *The Shyness and Social Anxiety Workbook*
    and *The Anti-Anxiety Workbook*

"Dr. Tompkins has done it again! In an increasingly stressful world, this book fills a key gap in the literature, and will undoubtedly be of great help to many youth and families."

Eric Storch, PhD
McIngvale Presidential Endowed Chair & Professor
Vice Chair & Head of Psychology
Department of Psychiatry and Behavioral Sciences
    Baylor College of Medicine

"We are in a youth mental health crisis. In this book, Dr. Tompkins provides a practical, down-to-earth guide to help teens identify and cope with stress. This should be recommended reading for every high school student!"

Mary Fristad, PhD
Director, Academic Affairs and Research Development
Nationwide Children's Hospital Big Lots Behavioral
    Health Services
Professor Emerita, The Ohio State University

"In clear language—but never talking down to youth—Tompkins provides essential skills for self-evaluation and coping, in great demand for adolescents of all stripes. Clear as a bell; highly recommended."

Stephen P. Hinshaw
Distinguished Professor of Psychology, UC Berkeley
Author of *Another Kind of Madness: A Journey Through the Stigma and Hope of Mental Illness*

"If you could give your teen one book—let it be this one. This is an invaluable resource! So much more than a guide to fielding stress. It is a powerful and thoughtful roadmap for life that will provide a solid foundation for teens for years and years to come."

Tamar Chansky, PhD
Author of *Freeing Your Child from Anxiety* and *Freeing Your Child from Negative Thinking*

"With the publication of this top-notch self-help resource, Dr. Tompkins cements his place as a trendsetter in clinical work with teens."

Robert D. Friedberg, PhD, ABPP
Professor, Head of Pediatric Behavioral Health
Emphasis Area
Director, Center for the Study and Treatment
of Anxious Youth
Professor, Palo Alto University

"Teens—life is stressful. Some people deal with stress better than others. But EVERYONE can benefit from *Stress Less*. I highly recommend it!"

Judith S. Beck, PhD
President of Beck Institute for Cognitive Behavior Therapy
Clinical Professor of psychology in psychiatry at University
of Pennsylvania

$\int$TRESS

$\mathcal{L}$ESS

A Teen's Guide to a
Calm Chill Life

MICHAEL $\mathcal{A}$. TOMPKINS, PhD, ABPP

Magination Press • Washington, DC • American Psychological Association

For Madeleine & Olivia

Books for Kids From the
American Psychological Association
maginationpress.org

Magination Press is a registered trademark of the American Psychological Association. Order books at maginationpress.org, or call 1-800-374-2721.

Cover design by Rachel Ross
Interior design by Circle Graphics
Printed by Lake Book Manufacturing, Inc., Melrose Park, IL

Library of Congress Cataloging-in-Publication Data

Names: Tompkins, Michael A., author.
Title: Stress less : a teen's guide to a calm chill life / Michael A. Tompkins, PhD, ABPP.
Description: Washington, DC : Magination Press, 2023. | Includes
    bibliographical references and index. | Summary: "Stress Less teaches
    concrete skills for managing stress and anxiety, organized into common
    "stress domains" such as family, friends, dating, school, and media"--
    Provided by publisher.
Identifiers: LCCN 2022024548 (print) | LCCN 2022024549 (ebook) |
    ISBN 9781433837043 (hardcover) | ISBN 9781433837050 (ebook)
Subjects: LCSH: Stress in adolescence--Juvenile literature. | Stress management
    for teenagers--Juvenile literature.
Classification: LCC BF724.3.S86 T66 2023 (print) | LCC BF724.3.S86 (ebook) |
    DDC 155.9/042--dc23/eng/20220609
LC record available at https://lccn.loc.gov/2022024548
LC ebook record available at https://lccn.loc.gov/2022024549

Manufactured in the United States of America
1 2 3 4 5 6 7 8 9 10

TABLE OF CONTENTS

Note to the Reader

Let's get real. Stress is part of every teen's life, and that's not changing any time soon. There's the stress of exams, college applications, a big game, difficult teachers, difficult friends, parents who don't always get you, not to mention the dating and social scenes. Stress like this tends to build over time—week after week—and takes a toll on your mental health. You feel overwhelmed, anxious, or down. You don't sleep well or enough; either too little because you're too stressed to settle down at night, or too much because sleep is the only escape from the stress. Stressed teens have chronic headaches or stomach aches and often binge on all the wrong foods. They're often irritable and take it out on their parents, or their siblings, or their friends. Yes, stress is serious business.

Is This Book for You?

If you're reading this book, it's likely someone who cares about you thinks you might be stressed, and that someone might be right. Teens report that their stress levels during the school year are much higher than they believe is healthy.[1] And their

---

[1] 2017 Stress in America Survey, American Psychological Association, November, 2017.

stress levels are higher than the stress levels of adults! If you're stressed, the skills in this book will help. In fact, they can help you even if you're not stressed. The strategies in this book are similar to those you might learn in cognitive-behavior therapy (CBT), a type of psychotherapy that helps with stress, anxiety, and other kinds of tough situations.

This book will not, however, take the place of counseling. Some teens benefit from the added support of a counselor as they learn and practice stress-busting skills. A counselor can also help you select the skills that are the best fit for you and for what you're dealing with in your life. Speak to your parents if you think a counselor could help you.

How to Use This Book

In Chapter 1, we'll talk about what stress is and how stress makes your life hard. It's not always as obvious as you might think! You'll then learn a model that breaks strategies down into skills for the *inside* and skills for the *outside*. Inside skills help you calm your stressed body and stressed mind, and outside skills help you manage the stressful situations or circumstances that come up in your life. You'll also meet a series of stressed teens and hear their stories. These *stress success stories* appear throughout the book.

In Chapter 2, you'll figure out the particular way stress affects you. You'll learn the ABCs of stress, which can help you recognize the first signs of stress so you know when to use the stress-busting skills in the book.

Chapters 3 to 8 are organized into six areas of life that tend to stress teens the most: school and work; performance and tests; family and friends; dating and relationships; media and technology; and health and hormones. You'll learn skills to manage stress in each of these specific areas.

Finally, in Chapter 9, you'll discover that there's more to life than just busting stress. Feeling happier and more confident are important, too. In this final chapter, you'll learn skills to increase your happiness and self-confidence.

The skills in this book aren't just for teens. That's because stress doesn't go away when you hit adulthood—there's stress galore then, too: a new college, a new job, a new relationship. The skills you'll learn and practice now will help you maintain your balance as you deal with the ups and downs of life in the months and years to come.

As you read through the book, you'll see the following features:

TRY IT features present the skill and how to use it. As mentioned, some skills are *inside* skills. Inside skills are great for calming your body and mind, such as slow deep breathing, meditation, or calm thinking. Then there are *outside* skills for managing the outside world, such as problem solving, communication, or managing time.

TRY IT HERE TOO features remind you that the stress-busting skill you learned can work for stress in another area. For example, the communication stress-busting skills in Chapter 6 (Dating and Relationship Stress) can help with family and friend stress (Chapter 5). Similarly, the assertiveness stress-busting skill in Chapter 5 can help with dating and relationship stress.

STRESS HACK features present brief and simple hacks that add to the stress-busting skill you learned. Sometimes the hack is a variation of the skill you just learned, and other times it's a twist on the skill. For example, the "hit the repeat button" technique is a great addition to the assertiveness skill you'll learn.

IN A NUTSHELL summarizes the main points of the chapter to help you remember what you've learned.

STRESS SKILL QUICK LOCATER. This table is at the end of the book and lists the six stress areas, all the stress management skills in the book, and the page numbers where you can find the skill quickly when you need it.

Getting Started

The skills in this book are easy to learn, but like any skill, whether it's riding a skateboard or playing a piano, it takes some practice to master them. I know what you're thinking: *Where will I find the time? I'm already over-booked and over-worked. Where will I find another minute to learn and practice something new?* I've got great news: Learning these stress-busting skills doesn't take much time at all. Twenty minutes per day is probably all it takes. You can learn on the bus, before bed, or during lunch. Once you learn one skill and see that it helps, you'll likely want to learn another. Learning is like that. You learn one thing and then you learn another; you make one change and then you make another. And before you realize it—you've got it!

GOOD LUCK!

MICHAEL A. TOMPKINS

*C*HAPTER 1

Stress Basics

Teens are more stressed than ever these days. That's because the world they're growing up in is far more complex, challenging, and fast-paced than the world their parents grew up in. Maybe you're stressed about a big test that's coming up, but you have to find time to work on college applications and finish two or three hours of homework per night too. Maybe you're stressed by a difficult conversation with your best friend, or with your parents who expect you to act like an adult but sometimes treat you like a kid. Maybe you're stressed that your social media posts aren't getting many likes or that you're not invited to a party that your friends are going to. Or maybe you're stressed about the "big" questions that parents, teachers, and even friends ask you: "Are you going to college?" "What's next for you?" "Are you happy?" Or the "big" questions you ask yourself: "Who am I?" "What's really important to me?" "Will I find a good job?"

What Is Stress?

Stress is your body's reaction to life's challenges. Of course, the ultimate life challenge is to survive a threat to life or limb, such as jumping out of the way of a charging rhino. This is the "fight, flight, or freeze" response, and is the stress response at its best. In an instant, you'll either fight back to defend yourself, run away if you can, or if you can't run away, you'll freeze. Fortunately, most teens don't face charging rhinos, but they do face daily hassles: tests, homework, arguments with friends, and conflicts with parents and teachers, to name a few. Daily hassles contribute the most to chronic stress. This is the stress that builds over the days and weeks and, if you don't do something to decrease it from time to time, causes all sorts of problems for you. Of course, there's the stress of major life events too, such as moving to a new school, the death of a much-loved pet, facing a serious illness, or a parent who loses a job. Although these major life events are stressful, they don't tend to contribute to the chronic stress that you want skills to cope with. That's because major life events like these don't come along too often, but life's hassles do.

The Positive and Negative of Stress

Not all stress is bad. In fact, life without stress would be pretty boring, unrewarding, and uninspiring. That's because most stress is the *positive* kind of stress. It motivates us to take on new challenges and to learn new things about ourselves and the world. For example, the excitement you feel on a first date. That's good stress because that kind of stress will help you make a great impression. The exhilaration you feel riding a roller coaster or trying new jumps in the skateboard rink. That's good stress, too. Good stress makes life exciting, fun, and helps us do our best.

The *negative* kind of stress, on the other hand, tends to overwhelm us and decrease our motivation and self-confidence. That's because negative stress tends to be chronic stress. Not only is it too high, but it stays high too long. Negative stress creates all kinds of problems. For example, sometimes stress is all over your face; acne can be a sign that you're under a lot of stress. Of course, other things can affect acne—hormones, excess oil production, and how much you touch your face—but stress doesn't help. And if you get stressed about your acne, then you're trapped in a vicious cycle: stress, acne, stress, acne.

Also, negative stress can make it difficult for you to get the sleep you need. You're up late trying to finish your work and then you lie in bed for hours unable to settle down and sleep when you're ready. Then, because you're tired the next day, everything is more difficult: studying, concentrating in class, tolerating your little sister, or performing well in soccer practice.

After a while, chronic stress and too little sleep get to you. You become more irritable. Little things set you off and you argue with friends. Soon, your friends don't want to hang out with you as much. Then life gets really hard, because your friends not only make life fun but they help you get through stressful days and weeks—when they're not around, it's even tougher to cope! Here are a just a few more problems negative stress can cause:

- Sadness, nervousness, worry, and panic
- Headaches, stomachaches, and frequent colds and infections
- Difficulty sleeping, nightmares, and disturbing dreams
- Fatigue, tiredness, and loss of motivation
- Difficulty focusing, concentrating, and making decisions
- Trouble learning, remembering, and memorizing new information
- Increased or decreased appetite, weight gain or loss
- Anger, irritability, and low tolerance for frustration

Positive and Negative Coping

Coping is using the skills you have to solve or tolerate life's challenges and not feel too distressed, anxious, or upset as you do it. Coping doesn't mean that you face life's challenges without feeling something. Sometimes people think that if they're feeling anxious or stressed, then they're not coping. That's not true. In fact, it's difficult to imagine not feeling stressed by a problem or challenge, and as you just learned, some stress helps you focus, think, and act in helpful ways. The goal of coping is to lessen the stress you feel while you solve the challenges you face.

When you're feeling stressed, particularly the kind of stress that goes on and on, day after day, it's natural that you want to do something to lessen it. Some of the ways to lessen stress are positive and healthy, like the skills in this book. Other ways to cope with stress are less healthy because they can negatively affect you and your life.

Also, negative coping is typically a quick fix to stress. Like most quick fixes, it only lasts for an hour or perhaps half a day, but soon you're back to the same level of stress or even more. There's more stress because you now have to deal with the big-time consequences that negative coping can create: unhappy parents, bad grades, or damaged friendships. Although the quick fix of negative coping works in the short term, it tends to harm you, your future, and the friends and family who care about you. There are lots of negative coping strategies, but here are the ones many teens use:

- *Eating too much or too little*: Emotional eating is eating to escape stress and other difficult feelings. You might eat to get your mind off things that are bothering you. You might eat to bury hurt or sadness, or when you're feeling bored or lonely. Sometimes teens try to control their stress by controlling how much they eat. Other times, teens lose their appetites when they're feeling too stressed or anxious. If you're eating too little or too much, reach out to a caring adult for help. Emotional eating is a sign that your stress is too high.
- *Exploding in anger*: When stress builds day after day, you might explode with anger and say and do mean things. If you're stressed about a school essay that's due tomorrow and you're running out of time to complete it, you might throw your book across the room.

You might scream rather than giggle at your brother when he burps at the dinner table. You might roll your eyes at a friend because she has an irritating laugh, although most days you think her laugh is funny. Anger isn't a great way to deal with stress because anger tends to create more and bigger problems for you. You can lose friends, miss important opportunities, or even get yourself expelled from school.

- *Stepping back from life*: Some people deal with stress by stepping back from life. They avoid their responsibilities in order to escape stress and anxiety. Spending time alone in your room because you're too stressed to deal with friends, family members, and the pile of homework on your plate only makes stress worse.

- *Using screens too much*: Screens are an easy way to escape from stress and anxiety. After all, it's easy to grab your phone or another device and chill for an hour or two or three or four, or binge-watch show after show, or play video games into the early morning hours. Too much time on screens, however, makes it difficult for you to get things done, to meet deadlines, and to grow as a person.

- *Using drugs and alcohol*: Some people use drugs and alcohol to escape from stress and anxiety. If you're using drugs and alcohol to deal with stress, anxiety, or even sadness, it's a signal that your stress is too high and that your ability to cope with it is too low. Drug and alcohol use is truly a short-term fix for stress that will only make your life more difficult, more stressful, and less fun.

- *Hurting yourself*: This is when stress gets dangerous. Some people deal with stress by cutting or hurting themselves in some way. Hurting or thinking about hurting yourself is a sign that you're stressed beyond your ability to cope. If you're thinking of suicide or of hurting yourself in any way, immediately speak to your parents, your doctor, a mental health professional, or call the National Suicide Prevention Life Line at 1-800-273-8255.

POSITIVE VS. NEGATIVE COPING SKILLS

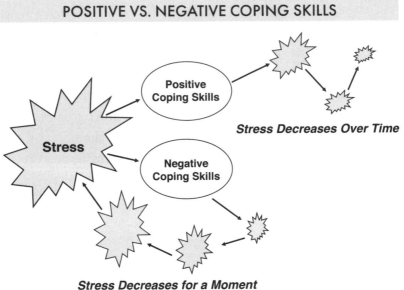

Positive
Coping Skills

Stress Decreases Over Time

Stress

Negative
Coping Skills

Stress Decreases for a Moment
but Increases Over Time

If you cope with stress in negative ways, it's not your fault. People often cope in negative ways because they haven't learned positive ways. That's how this book can help. It's filled with positive coping skills to help you.

Now that you know what stress and coping really are, it's time to take a deeper look at what causes stress and how the skills in this book can help you cope with it.

Outside and Inside of Stress

Have you ever wondered why tests stress out some of your friends but not others? Or why some friends freak out after a disagreement with a friend, but other friends are cool and calm? Well, what is or isn't stressful comes down to two things: the outside and the inside of stress.

Outside of Stress

You can't have stress without challenges, and you encounter challenges every day. This is the outside of stress: tests, meeting new people, breakups, sports competitions, and arguments with friends, to name a few.

The outside of stress is important, but what's outside (those activities, events and interactions) doesn't explain why these situations stress out some people a lot but don't stress others much at all. The answer is that stress is always the result of the interaction between outside and inside. That's why it's important to have stress-busting skills for both.

Inside of Stress

Now, stress isn't just about the test, the conflict, or the big game. How you think about the challenge affects how stressed you feel, which is the inside of stress. The inside of stress includes two evaluations or assumptions about any event or situation:

- **It's a threat**: If you think an event or situation is a danger or a threat to your well-being, then you'll feel stressed. For example, one person feels stressed if she thinks that she's a failure because she couldn't make a relationship work, but another person doesn't feel stressed because she thinks that she's free from a relationship that wasn't working for her. Also, the degree of threat depends on how big a stake you believe you have in how something turns out. For example, if you believe that your life is over if you don't get into the college you want, then you'll likely feel intensely stressed by the college application process. However, if you believe that you'll have a good life regardless of the college you attend, then you'll feel less stressed.

- **I can't handle it**: When you think that a situation or event is beyond your ability to handle it, then you'll feel more stress when you face it. For example, consider Lois and Brad, who are in line to receive their flu shot. They both know that the flu shot will hurt, but as Brad stands in line, he thinks, "I can't handle pain. It's too much for me." Lois, on the other hand, thinks that while the flu shot will hurt, she can handle it. Although Brad and Lois will likely feel the same level of pain, Brad will feel far more stressed and anxious about the flu shot than Lois.

Outside and Inside Stress Coping Skills

Now, let's get to the real reason you're reading this book. You want to learn to cope better with the stressful situations you face every day. To cope better, it's important that you learn skills to manage both the outside and the inside of stress:

- *Outside Coping Skills*: Outside coping skills help you change the environment or situation in some way. For example, clear communication is an outside coping skill because clear communication can change a stressful conversation with a friend (an outside situation) into a conversation that strengthens the friendship rather than damaging it. Similarly, skills to break down tasks, to manage time, and to solve problems all focus on changing the outside situation (tasks, time, problems).

- *Inside Coping Skills*: Inside coping skills help you change your emotional reaction to outside situations. For example, relaxation skills such as visualization or slow deep breathing can help calm your stressed body. Thinking skills can shift the way you think about situations to lessen the stress you feel.

OUTSIDE AND INSIDE MODEL OF STRESS AND COPING

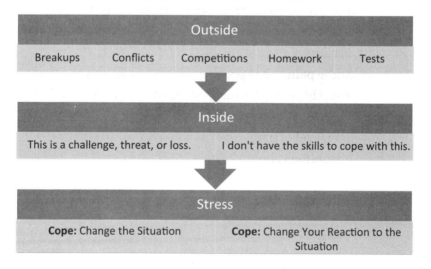

The next section describes the basic types of outside and inside coping skills that appear throughout the book. Often, there are several skills in a basic skill type. For example, clear communication skills, such as assertiveness, resolving conflict, and negotiating, all focus on decreasing stress by improving your interactions with other people.

Outside Stress Skills

Outside stress skills help you change the environment in some way. As you learn and practice skills to handle life's bumps and challenges, whether it's a loss of a best friend, an upcoming big game or test, or a ton of homework, you'll feel better prepared,

OUTSIDE AND INSIDE STRESS COPING SKILLS

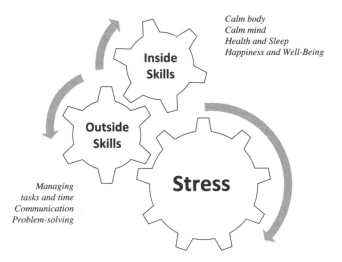

more confident, and therefore less stressed. Here are the types of outside stress coping skills:

Managing Tasks and Time Skills

One of the biggest stresses for teens is too many things to do and not enough time to do them. Therefore, skills to manage tasks and time are essential stress coping skills. For example, dividing large tasks into smaller tasks decreases your stress but it also decreases the likelihood that you'll put off starting tasks until the last minute. And speaking of time, skills that help you schedule your time and accurately estimate the time a task will take help you manage the time you have effectively. You'll learn additional outside skills in this category, such as skills to manage distraction, to procrastinate less, to stay on top of your social media and device use, and to schedule your activities throughout the day (including time to sleep!).

Communication Skills

As important as friends and family are to most teens, these relationships can be stressful too, particularly if you lack effective communication skills. Good communication skills will also help you to stand up for yourself, negotiate, and de-escalate conflict, which will help you feel less stressed and more confident in your interactions with friends, family, teachers, boss—you name it! Communication skills also include things like how to take feedback, forgive, and set healthy boundaries.

Problem-Solving Skills

Nothing is more stressful than having a problem that you don't know how to solve. As a busy teen, you likely encounter problems every day and often all day long: big problems, small problems, and problems in between. Whether it's a problem with a friend, with a teacher, or how to find time to complete an essay, problem-solving skills are an essential set of outside skills to include in your stress-management toolbox.

Inside Stress Skills

Inside skills change your emotional reaction to outside events and challenges. Your emotional reaction includes your stressed thoughts and your stressed body. Therefore, inside stress management skills include calm body skills and calm mind skills:

Calm Body Skills

Calm body skills focus on calming your stressed body. Because different people benefit from different calm body skills, it's important to have a variety of them to try. These can include things like progressive muscle relaxation, slow deep breathing, and positive imagery, to name a few. Try all the calm body skills in the book at least once and then pick one or two that work best for you. To benefit fully from the skill, practice it often. It takes practice to master anything, and coping skills like these are no exception. Also, the more tense, revved, or stressed your body is, the more practice it may take to feel the full benefit of the calm body skills.

Calm Mind Skills

Calm mind skills focus on calming the thoughts that fuel your stress. Calm mind skills include mindfulness skills and thinking skills:

Mindfulness Skills. Stress is often about the future or about the past. It's about something bad that could happen that hasn't happened yet, or it's about something bad that happened in the past but there's nothing you can do to correct it. A test tomorrow. A big game next week. A first date that didn't go well. If stress is time in the future or time in the past, then the antidote for stress is time in the present moment. Minding the present moment means to be aware. This is mindfulness. Mindfulness includes two key intentions:

- **Mindfulness is nonjudgmental**. When you're mindful, your intention is to observe without interpreting, evaluating, or criticizing.
- **Mindfulness is focused on the present moment**. When you're mindful, your intention is to see, hear, and feel what's happening now, rather than what might happen in the future, or what might have happened in the past.

Now, minding the present moment doesn't come naturally to people. Our minds don't work that way. Our minds, by nature, take us into the future or into the past. And this natural tendency is generally helpful. Our mind's ability to anticipate problems or threats in the future protects us from the real dangers and difficulties we face in our lives, and it helps us learn what worked or didn't work in the past so that we can be more effective and prepared in the future. However, just because minding the present moment works against your mind's natural tendency, it doesn't mean you can't learn to do this. It just takes some practice.

Thinking Skills. What we think and say to ourselves is called *self-talk*, and it's the way we interpret situations. How we interpret a situation determines how we feel and act. Your mind has the capacity to generate many types of self-talk, and each type of self-talk can be helpful, neutral, or unhelpful. For example, when your math teacher announces a pop quiz, if you think instantly, "I'm going to flunk the quiz. I'm horrible at math. I don't know what I'm doing," your stress spikes and you begin to sweat and have trouble concentrating and remembering what you studied. This is unhelpful self-talk because your stress is high enough that it might affect your performance on the quiz. However, if you think, "I probably won't flunk the quiz, but even if I do, it's just a pop quiz. My math grade is still pretty solid. I did my math homework and even though I'm not the best at math, I know enough to at least pass a pop quiz," your stress remains low. This is helpful self-talk because your stress is low enough that you can concentrate on the quiz, remember what you studied, and try to do your best. Therefore, how you think about an event and about your ability to handle the event can push your stress up or down. Unfortunately, stressed teens tend to have a pattern of self-talk that creates high levels of stress.

Health and Sleep Skills

Stress can affect both your health and sleep. Health and sleep skills focus on improving both. In fact, not only does stress affect your health and sleep, but the effects of stress on your health and sleep tend to increase your stress level. For example, if you're stressed about a big exam on Friday, you might sleep poorly the entire week leading up to the exam. By the day of the exam, you're so tired that you're having trouble concentrating and remembering what you studied. As you realize that you're having trouble concentrating in the exam, your stress builds and builds. It's a vicious cycle: stress, poor sleep, more stress, poorer sleep. Similarly, stress can affect your health: headaches, stomach aches, acne, or hair loss, to name a few. Health and sleep skills include skills to improve sleep, nutrition, and exercise.

Happiness and Well-Being Skills

Teens with low self-esteem and low self-confidence are more vulnerable to stress. So skills to increase self-esteem, self-confidence, and positive relationships are important. These skills will not only decrease your stress, but they'll also increase your happiness and contentment. Skills that focus on gratitude, self-compassion, and self-acceptance create a life that is meaningful and fulfilling. Happiness and well-being skills include, for example, loving kindness and gratitude meditations, ways to increase self-acceptance and balance in your life, and ways to increase hopefulness and a positive view of you and your future.

Typical Areas of Teen Stress

Although everyone feels stressed from time to time, not everyone feels stressed about the same things and in the same way. There are some typical areas that stress most teens. The chapters of this book focus on these areas. You'll learn a variety of skills to deal with stress in each area, and many of the skills will help in more than one area.

School and Work Stress

School and work are perhaps the biggest source of stress for most teens. Too many things to do and not enough time to do them. Teens feel pressure to get good grades and squeeze in time for fun, too. They have homework every school night and most weekends, and if they have a job, they have to fit that in, too. They have to navigate difficult conversations with teachers, bosses, and parents. They have to give class presentations or participate in group projects. They have to prepare for job interviews and think about college and their futures.

❝ School work is piling up and I'm stressing out. I know what to do but I'm not doing it. I'm procrastinating. Every time I sit down to work, I feel overwhelmed. Then I make up reasons to put off starting: I'm too tired now. I'll do a little more research first. I'll watch one more video and then start. You name it! I'm falling farther and farther behind. The more I procrastinate the more stressed I feel and the more difficult it is for me to concentrate or even think. I know that school stresses out other kids too, but I'm miserable. I've got to learn how to calm down a little. I know that if I was less stressed I'd do better in school. But it's a vicious cycle! I'm too stressed to start my homework but I'm too stressed to not start it.
—Deion **❞**

Performance and Test Stress

For many teens, the things they love to do are the same things that stress them out. Whether it's a soccer game, a piano recital, or a school play, performances like these are often stressful. Then add tests—small tests like the Spanish pop quiz or big ones like the SAT—to the mix, and most teens move from one stressful performance or test to the next.

> " This Saturday is the big game and I'm totally stressed. I haven't been on top of my shots and my passes aren't great either. This is the big game and I can't make any mistakes—not a single one. The stakes are too high. Coach says I'm too hard on myself, and that I'm playing fine, but it doesn't feel that way. What if I miss a shot or turn over the ball? My teammates will never forgive me. I'll never forgive myself. I've never felt this stressed out about a game. I love basketball but if I don't get a handle on my stress, I might quit.
> —Asif "

Family and Friend Stress

Friendships are very important, but they're often fraught with stress and hurt feelings. Teens worry that they're not smart enough, attractive enough, or cool enough to fit in. They often have to deal with cliques and bullying, and with friends who pull away or lean too much on them. Family can be stressful, too. Teens have to deal with their parents' expectations, or at times their parents' divorce or separation. They may have to deal with a difficult sibling, or even the death of a much loved grandparent.

> " I won't lie; it's been a stressful year. My family moved after my first year of high school and I lost

all my friends. It's never been easy for me to make friends, but moving to a new school has made it ten times harder. My new school is huge, and I don't know anyone. And then there are all the cliques. Everyone already has friends! I've reached out to a couple of girls, and they were nice but no one is texting me. I dread school now and that's new for me. I used to love to go to school and see my friends. Now I'm so stressed that I can't sleep, and I'm binging on junk food at night. This only makes me more stressed because then I start to worry about how I look. It's my worst nightmare, but I don't know what to do. I feel overwhelmed and lost.

—Lois

"

Dating and Relationship Stress

Most teens are new to dating, and their first serious intimate relationship often begins during their teenage years. Many will have to deal with a broken heart, or perhaps deal with breaking the heart of someone else. Dating and intimate relationships are often stressful, but building and nurturing intimate relationships is an important part of becoming a fully developed human being.

" My friends don't get why I'm so stressed out about Tim. They tell me to chill but I can't stop stressing about our relationship. Every time I text him and he doesn't reply instantly, I freak out. I'm convinced that sooner or later he'll dump me. The last break up

was horrible. I still get emotional when I think about my ex. Tim is much nicer and cooler than my ex, but I can't handle another break up. If I don't get a handle on my stress, Tim will dump me because I'm freaking out all the time. I'd dump me too.
—Ofelia

"

Media and Technology Stress

Most teens cannot imagine life without technology (or life before modern technology, for that matter). But media and technology often create a great deal of stress. There's social media and the relentless stress that comes from comparing yourself to friends and what they're doing, watching, and wearing, and feeling intense pressure to measure up. Smart phones, gaming, and engaging technology at your fingertips can also interfere with getting enough sleep and getting things done.

" My mom says that I'm addicted to my phone, and I think she's right. I've noticed that I feel more and more stressed when I see a post that one of my friends is hanging out with another of my friends. I start to worry that they don't like me anymore. Also, the news stresses me out these days. There's too much negativity in the world. And I've got FOMO too, you know, that fear of missing out thing. I constantly check social media posts from my friends, and every time I do, it just makes me feel more stressed and unhappy. I know I should stop, but when I try to stop, it never lasts long. My mom

is threatening to take away my phone because
I'm so miserable; but that would freak me out
too! I hate social media but I can't live without
it either. What do I do?

—Kanesha

99

Health and Hormone Stress

The teen years are a period of intense physical growth and development. Growth like this creates unique challenges for teens. They must deal with the stress that accompanies sudden and significant fluctuations in hormone levels, and hormones affect everything: sleep, concentration, mood, and appetite. Teens might have to deal with sleep patterns that don't match school bell times, or a brain that turns on when it's time to sleep. They have to deal with the stress of a dramatically growing physical body and find healthy ways to nourish it when time is in short supply.

66

No matter what I do, I can't get enough sleep.
And when I'm tired, everything gets harder. I can't
concentrate, I can't even think straight. I'm yelling at
friends. I'm dragging through the day. I'm spending
too long staring at a math problem rather than
working on it. This only makes my stress worse. I've
got to figure out a way to get more sleep.

—Alesandro

99

🌰 In a Nutshell

In order to understand how stress management skills can help you feel less stressed, it's important to understand the basics of stress and coping. Getting the basics out of the way now helps you focus on the stress management skills you'll learn and practice later:

1. *Stress* is your body's reaction to life's challenges. *Coping* is using the skills you have to solve or tolerate life's problems and not feel too stressed or anxious in the process.

2. The *inside and outside model of stress and coping* assumes that stress is the interaction between events you encounter in your environment and the way you think about these events. Coping is how you manage them.

3. *Outside stress skills* help lessen stress by changing the events and situations you encounter each day, and *inside stress skills* lessen stress by changing your emotional reaction to these events and situations.

CHAPTER 2
Stress and You

The first step in learning to handle stress is to figure out how stress affects you personally. Believe it or not, you have a lot more control over *you* than you do over the many things (tests, friendships, social media) that stress you. And learning the how and why of your stress will help you understand why it's important for you to learn skills to manage it.

In this chapter, you'll learn the ABCs of stress. Once you know the ABCs of stress, you'll learn your particular stress signals. Many teens are very aware of the physical signals of chronic stress: headaches, stomachaches, moodiness, and difficulty sleeping. But your mind sends signals too. It's important for you to become aware of all your stress signals so that you'll know when to use the skills in this book.

The ABCs of Stress

When you learned to read, you first learned your ABCs. In order to learn to read your stress, you'll start with the ABCs too. As you now know, stress includes factors outside you, such as the events and challenges that trigger your stress, and also factors inside you, such as your mind and body, and the actions you take to cope with your stress. The ABCs of stress is a simple way to describe the building blocks of stress and coping. The ABCs of stress include three parts:

A is for Antecedent

Antecedents are the situations and events that trigger your stress. The antecedents of stress differ from person to person, depending on who they are and their particular circumstances. For example, your best friend not replying to your texts or the person you're dating spending time with friends rather than with you might be antecedents of stress for you but not for others. A big English paper that's due tomorrow or news that a friend is dating an ex might be antecedents of stress for others but not for you. Also, antecedents of stress aren't just people and situations that occur in the present moment. If you remember or think about a past event, these memories or thoughts can be antecedents of stress too, even if the event isn't happening now. It's important that you know your particular antecedents of stress. Look at this list of typical stressful events and situations for teens. Which apply to you?:

Family (for example, your parents are divorcing or separating, your parents are arguing with each other or with you, you're having regular conflicts with your sibling)

School or academics (tests, grades, difficult teachers, you have a different learning style)

Friendships (regular conflicts with your friends, betrayals, loss of friendships, friends ask you to keep secrets)

Body image (you're overly concerned about your weight, height, hair, skin blemishes)

Romantic relationships (new relationship, recent breakup, complicated relationship, you have very different expectations for the relationship)

Bullying or cyberbullying (other people are repeatedly humiliating you in front of peers or adults, you're a target of hurtful comments or photos)

Peer pressure (others regularly pressure you to use drugs or alcohol, to have sex, or to take other risks)

Money or resources (your family doesn't have enough money to buy books, school uniforms, to attend school functions and clubs, to buy clothes and other things that would help you fit in with others)

Change (you're moving to a different house or school, a new sibling was just born, you lost your pet, a grandparent, or a close friend)

Identity (you're figuring out who you are and how you want to express, present, or define yourself)

B is for Basics

Now comes the basics: the basics of stress, that is. The basics of stress include stressed body, stressed mind, and stressed actions. The body and mind are deeply connected. Your body sends signals to your mind and your mind sends signals to your body, and your body acts in response to both. These three parts (body, mind, actions) work together to increase and maintain your stressful reactions to the challenges you face:

Stressed Body

When your body is stressed, you experience a variety of physical sensations. Your heart rate and breathing get faster, and you feel tense and fidgety. Soon, the stressed bod y is feeding the stressed mind and you're going around and around, faster and faster. A stressed body can make it difficult for you to settle down at night and sleep, or can cause you to become more easily frustrated. And then this body tension lingers, long after the initial rush of stress and anxiety has passed. This means that your stressed body is primed and ready to become stressed again, and quickly, over very minor things. Look at the list of typical stressed body signals for teens on the next page. Which apply to you?

Stressed Mind

Take a moment and recall an event that really stressed you out. Talk to yourself the way you talked to yourself then: "What if I flunk the test?" "What if I freak out and embarrass myself?" "What if I say something stupid and my friends dump me?" Are you feeling stressed yet, even a little? Isn't that interesting? Just hanging out with these thoughts can make you feel stressed all over again. Stressful thoughts fuel stressful feelings. This is a stressed mind at work. Now, imagine the event again and

TYPICAL STRESSED BODY SIGNALS

Frequent headaches	Panic attacks
Clenching jaw, grinding teeth, jaw pain	Difficulty breathing, catching breath, sighing
Stuttering, stammering	Chest pain, rapid pulse
Trembling hands, lips	Frequent urination
Neck or back pain	Constipation, diarrhea
Frequent colds, herpes sores, infections	Increased frustration, irritability, edginess
Ringing, buzzing in ears	Sad, depressed
Frequent blushing	Dizziness, faintness
Overreaction to little annoyances	Hair loss, acne
Insomnia, nightmares, disturbing dreams	Nervous habits, fidgeting, feet tapping
Difficulty concentrating	Cold sweats
Trouble learning new information	Making more mistakes
Forgetfulness, confusion	Frequent crying spells
Less efficient or productive	Persistent fatigue, tiredness
Increased or decreased appetite	Unintended weight gain or loss
Tingling in hands, feet	Dry mouth
Dry mouth	Heartburn, nausea
Rashes, hives, itching	Feelings of loneliness, worthlessness

throw in a few calming thoughts, such as, "Relax. I'll probably do fine on the test. I usually do," or "It's going to be okay. I'm not freaking out right now," or "I probably won't say anything stupid and even if I do, my friends like me and wouldn't dump me over something silly like that." What did you notice? Perhaps you learned a fact about stress and anxiety—or any emotion, for that matter. Certain thoughts can stress you out and other thoughts can calm you down. Because the body and mind are connected, skills to calm your stressed mind will calm your stressed body, too.

Stressed Actions

Stressed actions are the ways you *cope* with stress. As you learned in Chapter 1, there are helpful and unhelpful ways to cope with stress, and generally the unhelpful ways make your life harder and, yes, more stressful, because there's nothing more stressful than dealing with the consequences of unhelpful coping. For example, if you're stressed about a big test tomorrow and your boyfriend interrupts you while you're studying, you might scream at him. Now, you're stressed about the test *and* worried that your boyfriend will be mad at you. Or you might eat too much or too little when you're stressed. Now, you're upset and stressed about how you look. Or you try to distract yourself from the stressful things in your life by spending too much time on screens, and now you're stressed because you're not doing well in school. It's not your fault that you cope in unhelpful ways. You're just trying to get through stressful days as best you can. But just because you don't know helpful coping skills right now doesn't mean you can't learn them. That's where this book comes in. This book will help you replace the unhelpful actions with helpful skills, and these skills will make your life easier rather than harder. Look at the list of the signs of unhelpful coping on the next page. Do any of these sound like you?

C is for Consequences

Finally, unhelpful coping tends to create consequences for you. Consequences differ for each person and for each particular episode of stress, but often, it's because you either avoid doing something or try to lessen your stress through unhelpful habits, such as

SIGNS OF UNHELPFUL COPING

Binge-watching shows non-stop

Playing video games non-stop

Withdrawing from friends and family

Overeating or gaining weight

Undereating or losing weight

Sleeping too much or too little

Lashing out at friends and family

Taking up smoking or smoking too much

Taking illegal or unsafe drugs

Drinking excessive alcohol

Avoiding schoolwork or classes

Hurting yourself

Avoiding talking about the problem

Engaging in risky behavior (like driving fast)

Impulsive shopping, buying

Increasing social media use

alcohol, drugs, or over-eating. A consequence might be short-term, such as feeling guilty when you skip your best friend's piano recital because you're too stressed to attend, or fail a pop quiz because you put off studying. At other times, the consequences might be long-term, such as failing a class because you stay home sick too often when you're stressed, or losing friends because you're too stressed to hang out with them. These long-term consequences not only affect your day-to-day life, but they build over time until each day of your life is harder and more limited. If you have a long-term pattern of dealing with stress in unhelpful ways, then you likely have a life filled with long-term consequences:

Friends

Unhelpful coping can cost you friends. Has a friend ever said to you, "You're too stressed to be around," or, "Hey, I know you're stressed but I'm tired of you constantly bailing on me." Good friends might take your excuses once, perhaps even two or three times, but sooner or later they give up. They stop texting you because they know you'll say no, or they feel disappointed that you don't attend their games or school performances. And knowing your friends are disappointed in you can add to your stress and disappointment in yourself.

Family

Unhelpful coping is hard on your family, too. Your stress might exhaust your parents who have tried repeatedly to help you feel relaxed and confident. Your siblings might be upset at you because you're always stressed and irritable. Your family might be sad that you don't attend family events because you're too stressed. Your significant other might feel burdened by your over-dependence or be tired of making excuses for you when you're feeling too stressed to do something.

School and Work

Unhelpful coping can make it difficult to succeed in school. You might feel too stressed to study for tests (and then fail them), or too stressed to even attend school (and fall farther and farther behind). You might be too stressed to ask for a raise at work, or your boss passes you over for a promotion because they think that you don't have the confidence to handle more responsibility. Most importantly, think about the opportunities you've lost to learn, to have fun, or to have new and exciting experiences because your stress caused you to avoid this or that.

Embarrassment and Guilt

Unhelpful coping often leads to other feelings, such as embarrassment, disappointment, or guilt. You might feel embarrassed because your younger sister tries things that you won't. You might feel disappointed in yourself because you stayed up watching shows to distract yourself from your stress and now you're late to school. You might feel guilty that you don't hang out with your friends because you're too stressed or anxious.

Health

Unhelpful coping can have long-term consequences on your health, too. You might skip meals or eat fast food because you're too stressed to eat healthy. You might binge on ice cream and cookies when you're feeling stressed and now your skin is breaking out. You might bite your nails or pick your skin because of the stress.

Self-image

Years of unhelpful coping can change how you see yourself. After weeks and months, you start to lose confidence in yourself. You might think that you're a loser, weak, or a failure. You might think that you can't do things as well as other people or that you can't do much at all.

> **"** I never realized how many problems my stressed actions create for me. Well, the truth is, I knew there were problems but it was easier to ignore them or to blame other people or other things for my stress, like too much friend drama or too much homework. I hate to admit that my stress is out of control but I'm learning that ignoring my stress doesn't make it go away. The other day I told Mr. Morris, my favorite teacher, that I was tired of feeling so stressed out. He told me that admitting that I was stressed was a big step and that my life would get a lot easier once I learned how to manage my stress.
> —Kanesha **"**

ABCs of Stress Log

Now that you know the ABCs of stress, it's time for you understand your particular ABCs. You can use an ABCs of Stress Log to do this—here's a blank example, and you can make your own on a separate sheet of paper (or on your computer, or in your phone—whatever works for you!).

THE ABCs OF STRESS LOG		
Antecedent	(The thing that causes the stress)	
Basics of Stress	Stressed Body	(How your body shows stress physically)
	Stressed Mind	(The stressed thoughts you are having)
	Stressed Actions	(What the stress prompts you to do)
Consequences	(What happens because of your stressed actions)	

Scan Your Body and Mind for Stress

A body scan is a common activity in a lot of mindfulness practices, but it is also a super helpful way to figure out exactly how stress is affecting you. To scan your mind and body for stress, follow these steps:

1. Lie down in a comfortable place like on a carpeted floor, couch, or bed. Close your eyes. Although you may feel sleepy during this exercise, try to remain awake and aware of your body in the present moment.

2. Think back to a stressful situation. This is the antecedent of your stress. Who was there? What were you doing? What was happening around you? Allow yourself to feel the stress again.

3. Read and record the following script on your phone and listen to the recording while you do the exercise, or you can just do it as you read. During the exercise, notice what you feel in your body. Are your hands tingling? Does your face feel warm? Notice the thoughts or images that are going through your mind and body. Are you thinking, "What if I fail the big test?" or "What if my friends leave me?" Throughout the exercise, you'll notice that your mind wanders away from your body. When you notice your mind has wandered, gently acknowledge it, and then return your attention to the part of the body you were focusing on.

SCAN YOUR BODY AND MIND FOR STRESS

Step 1 Bring your awareness to your left foot. Scan your left foot for any sensations. Slowly become aware of any tension or discomfort. Slowly become aware of your thoughts. Notice any images. Notice all thoughts that flow through your mind while you remember the stressful event. Notice and remember these sensations and thoughts.

Step 2 Now scan your left calf. Notice and allow any sensations that may be present. Scan slowly, up through your thigh now. Allow yourself to feel any and all sensations. If you don't feel anything at the moment, that's okay. Just allow yourself to feel what you don't feel. Slowly become aware of your thoughts and images. Notice all thoughts that flow through your mind while you remember the event. Notice and remember these sensations and thoughts.

Step 3 When you become aware of tension or discomfort, or other intense sensations in a particular part of your body, notice and remember them, and then breathe in to the sensations to bring a gentle awareness to the sensations present in your body, without trying to change them. Now, become aware of your thoughts. Notice all thoughts and images that flow through your mind while you remember the event. Notice and remember these sensations and thoughts.

Step 4   Now scan for any sensations in your right foot, your calf, and thigh. Simply notice all sensations and feel what is happening. Continue to bring awareness and a gentle curiosity to the sensations in your right leg. Slowly become aware of your thoughts and mental images. Notice all thoughts that flow through your mind while you remember the event. Notice and remember these sensations and thoughts.

Step 5   Now focus on your stomach. Feel it rising as you inhale. Sinking as you exhale. Nice and slow. Remain aware of your stomach and notice any sensations in your stomach area. Bring a gentle awareness to any tightness or discomfort in your stomach and notice and remember any sensations there. Now, slowly become aware of your thoughts and images. Notice all thoughts that flow through your mind while you remember the event. Notice and remember these sensations and thoughts.

Step 6   Now scan for any sensations in your left hand and arm. Simply become aware of the different sensations and feel what is happening. Continue to bring awareness and a gentle curiosity to the sensations. Again, if you don't feel anything at the moment, that's okay. Now, slowly become aware of all thoughts and images that flow through your mind while you remember the event. Notice and remember these sensations and thoughts.

Step 7   Scan for sensations in your right hand and arm. Continue to bring awareness, and a gentle curiosity to the sensations. Slowly become aware of your thoughts. Notice any images. Notice all thoughts that flow through your mind while you remember the event. Notice and remember these sensations and thoughts.

Step 8   Come back to your chest. Continue scanning up and along your neck, and to your face. Feel the sensations in your jaw, and in your throat. Notice how the back of your head rests against the surface under you. Bring your awareness to the top of your head. Notice and remember any sensations there or in your jaw, neck, or throat. Slowly, as before, become aware of your thoughts as you remember the event. Notice all thoughts that flow through your mind and remember these sensations and thoughts.

Step 9   Now take a moment to notice how all your body parts are feeling. Let any sensations come to you. Just notice the sensation – warm, tingling, tight, heavy. Accept the sensation as it is. Bring your awareness to your full body. Slowly become aware of all your thoughts. Accept these thoughts as you become aware of your body and mind in this moment. Notice all thoughts that flow through your mind while you remember the event. Notice and remember any sensations in your body and thoughts in your mind.

Step 10 Continue to focus on your breathing as long as you like, noticing and remembering any sensations there, and noticing and remembering any thoughts and images.

After you've done a scan, enter what you discovered in the ABCs of Stress Log that you created. Record the stressful event that you imagined in the *Antecedent* section of the log and enter what you observed in your body and in your mind in the *Stressed Body* and *Stressed Mind* sections of the log. Also think back to the ways you coped with the stress. These are your *Stressed Actions*; enter those, too. Did you binge on junk food to cope with the stress? Did you watch one show after another to distract yourself? Last, think about the event and record any consequences that you remember. Did you feel guilty because you bailed out of the event? Did you bite your nails all day? Did you argue with your significant other again? Write what happened in the *Consequences* section of the log.

> **"** I never knew how stressed I really was until I started to pay attention. Now that I know my stressed body signals, I can sometimes do a little something that helps. For example, the other day, coach asked me to help put away the equipment after practice. I started to feel my jaw tighten. That's one of my body's stress signals. I decided

to tell him that I was feeling pretty stressed about a big exam tomorrow and asked him if I could help with the equipment next time so that I could get home to study. He thanked me for letting him know and told me I could help with the next few practices. I told him thanks and immediately felt a little less stressed.

—Asif

99

Stress Scale

Now that you know your body's first signs of stress, the next step is to learn to rate the level of stress you feel. Many teens ignore their stress until it builds into an overwhelming wave of panic. Learning to catch your stress when it's low helps you get ahead of it. That will help you use the stress skills early when they'll help the most.

To build your stress scale, grab a blank piece of paper and a pencil or pen. Draw a line down the middle of the page, from the top to the bottom. Next, mark 0 to 100 along the line, to make a scale. Now, think back to several stressful events. Try to remember times when you were feeling stressed. Try to choose times when you were feeling different levels of stress (100: extreme, 75: high, 50: moderate, and 25: mild) and when you were feeling calm (0: no stress at all). Then, write the stressed body signals you remember next to each stress level. It's okay to estimate if you can't remember exactly how it felt in the moment! You'll update your stress scale as you learn more about your stressed body signals. Look at Deion's *Stress Scale* to see how he did it.

Deion is stressed about his relationship with his girlfriend, Anya. He loves Anya and Anya loves him, but he worries non-stop that she's going to break up with him. Although Anya repeatedly

DEION'S STRESS SCALE

Stress Scale	Stressed Body Signals	
Extreme Stress (100)	Heart racing	Screaming
	Crying	Vomiting
High Stress (75)	Face flushed	Sweating
	Hands trembling	Nauseous
Moderate Stress (50)	Voice trembling	Butterflies
	Dry mouth	Restless
Mild Stress (25)	Irritable	Trouble concentrating
	Not hungry	Headache
Calm (0)	Relaxed	Friendly
	Laughing	Comfortable

tells him not to stress, he can't stop himself from texting her for reassurance or from getting angry when she doesn't respond to his texts immediately. Deion completed an ABCs of Stress Log with all the parts, including the consequences of the unhelpful stressed actions he uses to cope. He also guessed his stress level was about 55 and wrote that in the *Stressed Body* section.

Try to complete several ABCs of Stress Logs over the next few weeks. What stressed body and mind signals do you have? Although it may feel like every stress episode is different and it's all happening at once, your stress actually covers the same ground each time: antecedent, stress basics, and consequences. Understanding your particular ABCs of stress will help slow down the build-up of stress during the day because you know the parts and how they work together. Don't forget to rate the level of stress with the stress scale. Rating it each time can help you start to notice that your level is actually different each time. Learning that your stress is not always 100 out of 100—even though it might feel that way—can help you feel a little more hopeful that your life isn't always as hard or stressful as it seems.

DEION'S ABCs OF STRESS LOG

Antecedent	Anya isn't responding to my texts.	
Basics of Stress	**Stressed Body**	My face is red and burning. My hands are shaking a little. My stomach is tingly. 55
	Stressed Mind	Anya's had enough of me. She's breaking up with me. I know it!
	Stressed Actions	I text Anya's friends to see if they know where she is and why she's not returning my texts. I play video games instead of homework.
Consequences	Anya's friends are upset with me and tell me to chill. When Anya returns my texts, she tells me that she was working with her math tutor and couldn't text me back. She reassures me that we're still good but I can tell she's upset with me and tells me that she can't see me tonight because she has too much homework. I know that's an excuse but it's probably for the best. I'm sick to my stomach, and I'm stressed about the homework that's due. I really hate myself.	

66 I've learned that knowing my body and mind stress
signals helps me get ahead of my stress a little.
I never knew when my stress was building because
I wasn't paying attention until I was freaking out. Now
that I know my body and mind stress signals, I can
do a little something to relax. For example, the other
day, Anya didn't return my text immediately. I started
to feel butterflies in my stomach. That's one of my
body's stress signals. I noticed that I was thinking,

"She's had it with me," which is one of the stressed mind thoughts I have. I decided to take a few calming breaths. That helped me relax, and after a few minutes, Anya called me. She was driving her grandmother to a doctor's appointment and she couldn't text me back. She told me that she missed me and that she was looking forward to seeing me tonight. Knowing that I was stressed and what to do to relax helped a lot!

—Deion

99

🌰 IN A NUTSHELL

Everyone feels stressed from time to time, but no two people feel stressed in the same way. It may feel like your stress is in charge of you and of your life, and that there's nothing you can do about it. But learning to recognize your own particular stress signals and patterns can help you manage it.

1. The *ABCs of Stress* include the *antecedents* (events and situations that trigger your stress), the *basics* of stress (stressed body, stressed mind, and stressed actions), and the *consequences* of your stress.

2. There are short-term and long-term consequences of stressed actions, which are the unhelpful ways you cope with your stress. Unhelpful coping might help in the short-term but tends to create long-term problems that only add to the stress you feel.

3. Learning your unique ABCs of stress using the ABCs of Stress Log will help to unpack these experiences and is the first step to feeling more in control of your emotional reactions.

CHAPTER 3
School and Work Stress

School is the number one stress area for most teens. There are tests, homework, oral presentations, studying for the SAT, taking the SAT, you name it. Juggling all these balls isn't easy. And if you work a job or have extracurriculars or sports, too, that just adds more stress on top of stress. In this chapter, you'll learn the following inside and outside skills to deal with school and work stress:

- Breathe Slowly and Deeply
- Relax Your Body
- Relax and Refresh
- Identify Your Thinking Traps
- Catch It, Check It, and Change It
- Divide and Conquer
- Schedule Time
- Estimate Time Accurately
- Do It Now
- Make Good Decisions Quickly

Breathe Slowly and Deeply

Slow deep breathing is a great skill to calm any kind of stress, not just school and work stress. To practice slow deep breathing, get comfortable in a favorite chair or lie on the bed, uncross your legs and arms, close your eyes, and follow these steps:

1. Place one hand on your upper chest and the other hand just below your ribcage, which is about where your diaphragm is. This allows you to feel your diaphragm move as you breathe in and out.

2. Close your mouth and breathe in slowly through your nose for a slow count of 1-2-3. Think the word *CALM* to yourself as you breathe in. Feel your stomach move out against your hand as you inhale. Imagine your breath is going all the way down into your stomach and filling it up.

3. Hold your breath and slowly count 1-2-3-4 in your head.

4. Next, say the word *EASY* to yourself, and imagine the word in your mind's eye as you exhale through pursed lips, making a *whoosh* sound. Exhale for a slow count of 1-2-3-4-5-6-7. As you breathe, imagine the air traveling out of your lungs slowly and evenly. Pause.

5. Repeat this slow, deep, and rhythmic flow for a total of 10–15 minutes. If your mind wanders during the exercise, just refocus your attention on the image of the word *CALM* or *EASY* in your mind's eye and continue breathing in and out, noticing your chest rise and fall.

66 My band director and my soccer coach are pretty different people, but they do agree on one thing. They both told me that the breath is the path to calm. I didn't understand what they meant at first, but then I tried the breathe slowly and deeply skill a couple of times. It worked. I could feel my body calm down, slow down, and relax. It was easy to do too. Now, when I notice that I'm stressed before a test, or during a band rehearsal or even at the penalty area, I take a slow deep breath and walk down the path toward calm.

—Alesandro

99

-☀- *STRESS HACK:* If you're an athlete, you likely do resistance exercises to strengthen your skeletal and core muscles. The diaphragm is a muscle, too. The diaphragm tightens during inhalation, so a strong diaphragm reduces breathing effort and improves your performance. Alternate nostril breathing is another version of deep breathing exercises, and is a resistance training technique that strengthens your diaphragm. And it's easy to do. First, find a quiet spot where you won't be disturbed, sit upright, and close your eyes. Place your right thumb to block your right nostril and inhale for several seconds. Then, remove your thumb and block your left nostril with the first two fingers of your right hand and exhale. Repeat 10–12 times, or for longer if you wish.

-☀- *STRESS HACK:* Slow deep breathing shifts your nervous system to a more restful state by stimulating the vagus nerve, the longest nerve in your body. The vagus nerve connects your brain to many important organs throughout your body, including your heart, lungs, and intestines. Therefore, slow deep breathing sends a message to your brain and then your brain sends a message to your body to relax, to calm down, and to slow down. But there are other ways to stimulate this nerve. For example, and you may not believe this, but singing and humming also activate the vagus nerve. Even gargling can stimulate it. So, next time you're feeling stressed, hum or sing your favorite tune or gargle your orange juice.

RELAX YOUR BODY

Think of your body as if it's a balloon that fills with stress throughout the day. By the end of the day your body feels like it's about to explode from so much stress and pressure. That's because you didn't do anything to release stress from the balloon. The balloon just keeps filling and filling until it can't fill any more. Learning to relax your body is a great skill to release the stress from the balloon, but it's super important to do it every day. It's like an antidote for stress. You do it every day so that you start each new day with an empty stress balloon.

Progressive muscle relaxation helps release pent-up tension. Concert violinists repeatedly open and close their hands to relax them before they play. Professional basketball players shrug their shoulders or shake their heads before they take a free throw. These simple gestures release pent up tension, which helps muscles perform optimally. Just like musicians and athletes, you too can learn to relax your muscles and decrease the unwanted tension that's adding to your school or work stress, or other kinds of stress too. *Don't engage in this exercise if you have a medical condition that makes it unsafe for you to tense and relax your muscles.*

To practice relaxing your body, lie down with your arms by your side and your legs uncrossed and flat on the ground. Close your eyes and follow these steps:

1. Start by squeezing your eyes tight, scrunch your nose as if you've smelled a rotten egg, pull the edges of your mouth back toward your ears into a forced smile, and clench your teeth to tense your mouth and jaw. Hold this position as you count to 15 to yourself. Then slowly release your eyes, nose, mouth, and jaw. Relax your face so all the wrinkles disappear. Notice how different this feels from when your face was tight and tense. Hold this relaxed position as you count to 15.

2. Now, move to your neck and shoulders. Drop your chin to your chest and pull your shoulders up to your ears. Hold this position as you count to 15, observing the tension in your neck and shoulder muscles. Now release, let your shoulders drop down, and relax your head. Hold this relaxed position as you count to 15.

3. Next, move to your hands and arms. Make fists with your hands and cross your arms at the wrists. Hold your arms up in front of you and push them together as if you're arm wrestling with yourself. Hold your arms in this position with your fists clenched as you count to 15. Then let your fists uncurl and your arms slowly fall to your sides. Notice how your arms feel loose and heavy, and this feeling of relaxation feels much better than when your muscles were tense and tight. Hold this relaxed position as you count to 15.

4. Next, suck in your stomach, making your abdomen hard and tight, and clench your buttock muscles together. Hold this position as you count to 15. Notice how the tension feels uncomfortable. Then release and let your stomach go out further and further while you release your buttock muscles. Hold this relaxed position as you count to 15.

5. Last, tighten your leg muscles and point your feet toward your head while you scrunch your toes into a tight ball. Hold this position as you count to 15, then release and relax your feet and legs. Hold this relaxed position as you count to 15.

You might notice as you go through all these muscle exercises, tensing and relaxing, that you're starting to feel calmer. You feel grounded, as if you're melting into the floor. Your muscles might feel heavy and loose, and your whole body is beginning to feel relaxed. You're in charge of how your body feels, and you're commanding your muscles to relax. You can repeat these five steps to relax your body even more, beginning again with your eyes.

RELAX AND REFRESH

Believe it or not, you can talk yourself into a relaxing and refreshing state of mind. You simply tell yourself repeatedly to focus lightly on a feeling of warm heaviness in parts of your body. To relax and refresh, sit in an armchair or lie down on your back in a quiet room. Close your eyes or keep your eyes open and softly focus on a point in front of you. Take a few slow, deep, and relaxing breaths. Now, slowly say to yourself each of the following phrases three or four times:

> *My forehead and scalp are heavy, limp, loose, and relaxed.*
> *My eyes and nose are heavy, limp, loose, and relaxed.*
> *My face and jaw are heavy, limp, loose, and relaxed.*
> *My neck, shoulders, and back are heavy, limp, loose, and relaxed.*
> *My arms and hands are heavy, limp, loose, and relaxed.*
> *My chest and arms are heavy, limp, loose, and relaxed.*
> *My stomach and hips are heavy, limp, loose, and relaxed.*
> *My buttocks, thighs, calves, ankles, and toes are heavy, limp, loose, and relaxed.*
> *My whole body is heavy, limp, loose, and relaxed.*

This will take about 3–4 minutes. As you silently repeat each phrase, lightly focus your attention on that part of your body. Just notice what happens in that part of your body. If you record this, leave about 30 seconds of silence between each part.

At first, your attention will wander away from the relaxing and refreshing feeling growing in that part of your body. That's okay. Just return your attention to the relaxing and refreshing feeling. At the end of the practice, say to yourself, *When I open my eyes, I'll feel relaxed, refreshed, and alert.* Then, open your eyes and take a few deep slow breaths as you stretch and flex your arms and legs.

-☼- *STRESS HACK:* Try this stress release skill to de-stress quickly. It combines releasing muscle tension and visualization. Here's how it works. Grab two tennis balls, one in each hand. If you don't have tennis balls, use balled up wash cloths or socks. Now, close your eyes and squeeze the tennis balls as you imagine squeezing toothpaste out of a tube or juice out of a lemon. Squeeze as you count to 5, then release as you spread open your hands. Squeeze again as you count to 5, then release as you spread open your hands. Repeat three times. With practice, you'll bring on the relaxation response in a few seconds just by imagining squeezing the toothpaste or lemon and then spreading open your hands.

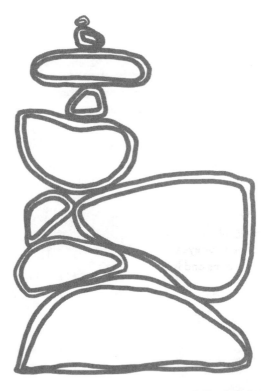

Thinking traps are unhelpful patterns of thinking that tend to trap you in stress and anxiety and make it difficult for you to see things as they really are. Some people fall into many thinking traps and others fall into just a few, but they all tend to fall into these traps over and over again. Some traps are about assuming the worst of other people. Other traps are about expecting that others will always treat you fairly. As you get to know the thinking traps, you'll realize that some of the traps overlap or seem similar. That's okay. It's not important whether you have just a few or many thinking traps, or how much they overlap. The most important thing is to become familiar with the ones that you tend to fall into. Knowing that you've slipped into a thinking trap can help you quickly jump out of it. This alone can help decrease the stress you feel. Here's a list of common thinking traps that fuel stress:

COMMON THINKING TRAPS

Thinking Trap	Description	Example
Being Right	You think you need to be right and you will go to any length to prove it.	"I don't care what the teacher said. She's wrong and I'm right!"
Black or White	You think in black or white with no shades of gray.	"If I don't get an A+ in this class then I'm a failure."
Doom and Gloom	You jump to negative conclusions before you have all the facts.	"They don't like me because they didn't invite me to the party."
Catastrophizing	You predict the worst and blow things out of proportion.	"If I don't get into Harvard, my life is over."
Fallacy of Change	You think that you can change people if you pressure them enough.	"He said no, but I'll still get him to go with me to the game."

Fallacy of Fairness	You think things should always be fair, although that's not the way the world works.	"It's not fair that she has a boyfriend and I don't."
Filtering	You focus on negatives while ignoring positives of situations.	"Yes, I got an A on the paper, but I still misspelled a word."
Fortune Telling	You think you can predict the future and typically predict the negative.	"I'm not going to get the part in the school play."
Heaven's Reward	You think that your sacrifice will pay off someday.	"If I'm nice to her no matter how mean she is one day she'll like me."
Mind Reading	You think you know what people think and why they do what they do.	"He's lying to make me feel better, but he really wants to break up."
Labeling	You put negative labels on yourself or on other people.	"I'm boring." "He's an idiot."
Overgeneralization	You draw conclusions based on a single event or piece of evidence.	"I got a C on this test, I'm terrible at math."
Personalization	You think that what people say or do, or what happens, is a reaction to you.	"It's my fault that we lost the game."
Should, Must	You have ironclad rules that you think you and others should follow.	"I must get good grades." "He should be on time."

Now try your hand at a brief Thinking Trap Test. Look at this list of situations (antecedents) and the stressed thoughts that the situations trigger. Select the thinking trap that best fits the stressed thought. Remember that several thinking traps might fit the same stressed thought. That's okay. Just select one that makes sense to you. The answers to the questions are at the bottom.

THINKING TRAP TEST

Antecedent (Trigger)	Stressed Thought	Thinking Trap
1. My boyfriend dumped me.	I'll never find someone who loves me.	_____
2. I'm struggling with this math problem.	I'm going to flunk this class.	_____
3. I stumbled over a few words during my presentation.	The other kids think I'm an idiot.	_____
4. I got a C+ on my final exam.	I'm a total loser.	_____
5. I made a bad pass in soccer.	I always do this. I can't play this game at all.	_____
6. I'm 5 minutes late to practice.	Coach is going to bench me for the rest of the season.	_____
7. Josh told me that he has to stay home tonight to study.	He said no but I'll get him to go out tonight.	_____
8. I didn't understand a question during my interview.	That was the worst interview I've ever done.	_____
9. I have an idea for a new floor exercise in my gym class.	The teacher is going to shoot down my idea.	_____
10. Jesus didn't like the video game we played.	It's my fault that Jesus didn't have a good time with me.	_____
11. I was invited to a party but have other plans with my mom.	I should go to the party even though I don't want to.	_____
12. My mom told me that I had to stay home and babysit Ana.	It's not fair that Mom told me that I couldn't go out tonight.	_____

Answers: 1. Black or White, 2. Doom and Gloom, 3. Mind Reading, 4. Labeling, 5. Filtering, 6. Catastrophizing, 7. Fallacy of Change, 8. Overgeneralization, 9. Fortune Telling, 10. Personalization, 11. Should, Must, 12. Fallacy of Fairness.

Now look at the list of thinking traps again. On a blank sheet of paper, write the name of the thinking traps you tend to fall into. Next to each thinking trap, write examples of the kinds of stressed thoughts you have.

> **66** There's a reason they call them traps. It's not easy to climb out of a thinking trap even when I know I've fallen into one. But I'm getting better at it. The other night I was feeling stressed about my audition the next day for the school play, until I realized that I'd fallen into the doom and gloom thinking trap. I was thinking that I was going to bomb the audition before I had even tried. Just realizing that I had fallen into the doom and gloom thinking trap helped me feel a little less stressed about the audition. And guess what? I got the part!
> —Ofelia **99**

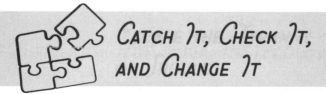

CATCH IT, CHECK IT, AND CHANGE IT

The 3Cs is an inside stress management skill that can help you catch and then change the thoughts that fuel your stress. The skill includes three parts: Catch It, Check It, Change It. To practice the 3Cs skill, follow these steps:

1. Take a blank sheet of paper and draw lines to make three columns. Label the left column *Catch It*, the middle column *Check It*, and the right column *Change It*.

2. In the *Catch It* column, write the stress thought. *Catch It* means that you catch the thought that fuels your stress. The best way to catch a thought is to check for thoughts when you're feeling stressed. Stress signals in your body are a hint that stressful thoughts are running through your mind. To catch the stress thought, ask yourself:
   - What am I thinking right now?
   - Is this thought making me feel stressed?
   - What images or pictures are running through my mind right now (for example, the image of me missing a free-throw shot)?
   - Does this image or picture make me feel stressed?

3. If several stressful thoughts are running through your mind, rate how strongly you believe each thought to be true (from 0 to 100, where 100 means you completely believe it to be true). The thought that you rate as most true is the thought that is most likely to fuel high stress. You'll focus on this thought because the stronger you believe a thought, the more intense the feeling associated with the thought.

4. *Check It* means checking to see if the stress thought is a thinking trap. Check the list of thinking traps. Remember, there's considerable overlap among thinking traps, so it's okay to identify all the traps that fit. In the *Check It* column, write the names of all the thinking traps that fit the stress thought.

5. *Change It* means that you'll change the stress thought into a calm thought. To change the thought, ask yourself the following questions:
   - Is the thought really true?
   - Is there another more helpful way to look at this?

- Do I have evidence that tells me it's true?
- How about evidence that the thought is false?
- Would a friend think about this event or situation in the same way?
- Does this thought make my life easier or more difficult?
- Is this thought helping or hindering my life goals?
- What's the worst negative outcome that could happen and how likely is that?
- What's the best outcome that could happen and how likely is that?
- What's the most likely negative outcome and what is my plan to handle it?

Questioning your thinking can be difficult because these thoughts are likely familiar and "feel" true. However, just because something feels true doesn't mean it is true. In the *Change It* column, write the calm thought or thoughts you came up with.

That's it. Look at what Deion and Kanesha came up with when they used the 3Cs skill to change their stressed thoughts to calm thoughts. They then repeated the calm thoughts to themselves the next time they were feeling stressed, and they could step back a little and see that things weren't as bad as they seemed in the moment.

DEION & KANESHA'S CATCH IT, CHECK IT, CHANGE IT EXERCISE

Deion

Catch It	Check It	Change It
Stress Thought	Thinking Trap	Calm Thought
If I don't get an A+ in this class then I'm a failure.	Black or White	I can be a success and not always get an A+. There's a lot more to me than grades, and even if I did get less than an A+, It doesn't mean that I'm a failure. It just means that I'm not perfect.

Deion Continued

Catch It	Check It	Change It
Stress Thought	Thinking Trap	Calm Thought
I'm not going to get the part in the school play.	Fortune Telling	I can't tell the future so I don't know whether I'll get the part or not. I do know that my chances are as good as anyone else and I've studied for the part and I'm ready.
I'm an idiot.	Labeling	This is harsh. Would I call a friend an idiot because he forgot something? I'm not an idiot but I'm not perfect either. Go easy on yourself.
I got an A on the paper, but it doesn't count because I misspelled a word.	Filtering	What about all the other words I spelled correctly? Take in the whole picture. Yes, I misspelled a word but that doesn't mean I don't deserve an A on the paper.
If I don't get into Harvard, my life is over.	Catastrophizing	Wow! What would I say to a friend who thought this? My life isn't over. Not every successful person in the world goes to Harvard. It's about me not the college!

Kanesha

Catch It	Check It	Change It
Stress Thought	*Thinking Trap*	*Calm Thought*
It's my fault that our team didn't win.	Personalization	Would I tell myself that me and only me won a game? No! That's because the team wins or the team loses and it's never just one person's fault.
My coach thinks I don't know what I'm doing.	Mind Reading	I can't read minds. I don't know what he's thinking. He hasn't said that I'm not doing well. In fact, he told me that I'm doing fine.
I'll never get promoted at work.	Doom and Gloom	I don't know that this is true. Assuming I won't get promoted just sets me up to feel bad. Why not assume I will? What do I have to lose?
I shouldn't have to do so much homework.	Should, Must	I don't want to do so much homework. Who does? But I don't make the rules, and thinking that I shouldn't have to do homework doesn't help me or change the fact that I have to do it if I want to do well in school. Which I do!

" The Catch It, Check It, Change It skill puts everything together. Catching my stress thoughts is the first step and probably the most important. I can't calm down if I don't know what I'm thinking that's stressing me out! Then checking if the stress thought is a thinking trap is a quick way to reset my mind. What's the point of stressing if what I'm thinking doesn't make any sense to begin with? The last step helps too. Changing my stress thoughts into calm thoughts takes some time, but I've noticed that I'm feeling less stressed about school and work. I guess I'm teaching myself to think differently about things and it's helping.

—Deion "

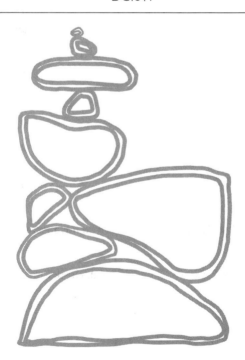

DIVIDE AND CONQUER

When you're stressed, it can be difficult to start and finish schoolwork, homework, or college or job applications, and things that aren't getting done only add to your stress. Small tasks that you could whip through without a second thought can seem huge and overwhelming when you're stressed. Furthermore, the bigger the project or more complex the task, or the more difficult or boring it is, the more likely you are to procrastinate starting it. Dividing a task or project into smaller parts is a great skill to conquer tasks that you're avoiding starting. That's because the smaller the part, the more likely you are to start it. Plus, completing a small part or step motivates you to try the next one. That's because you completed something and the satisfaction (and relief) of that makes it easier to start the next step. Soon you're on a roll and you can see the light at the end of the tunnel. Follow these steps to divide and conquer:

1. Think of a project that's stressing you out and that you're putting off starting. It could be a school project, home project, or even a friend project (for example, making a birthday card for your best friend).

2. Rate (0 to 100 where 100 is extremely stressed) the stress you feel about the task or project that you're having trouble starting.

3. Now, ask yourself, "How many parts can I divide this task into?" Then, divide the task or project into as many small steps as you can think of.

4. Then, look at each step. Rate the level of stress (0 to 100) you feel if you try the step the way you described it. Try for a stress level of 30 or less. If your stress is more than 30, break that small step into a couple of smaller steps.

5. Keep breaking down each step until you have steps with stress levels of 30 or less.

To see how to divide and conquer a project, check out Lois's *Divide and Conquer*.

LOIS'S DIVIDE AND CONQUER

Step 1: Describe the task or project that you want to divide and conquer:

Write a three page essay on the impact on sea level of climate change.

Step 2: Rate your stress level (0 to 100) with the stress scale:

Stress = 90

Step 3: Divide the task into at least six small steps and rate the level of stress you think you'll feel for each step:

1. Research the topic. Stress = 30
2. Create an outline. Stress = 20
3. Write the first draft. Stress = 50
4. Dad reads first draft and adds his suggestions. Stress = 20
5. Write a second draft. Stress = 30
6. Check grammar, for typos, and write final draft. Stress = 20

Step 4: If the stress level for a step is greater than 30, break that step into smaller steps:

3. Write the first draft. Stress = 50
   a. Write topic sentence for each topic in outline. Stress = 20
   b. Write paragraph of each outline topic. Stress = 30
   c. Review and complete first draft of each paragraph. Stress = 10

TRY IT HERE TOO: Divide and conquer can help you start and complete many other projects and tasks, not just homework or job applications. Divide and conquer works with fun but big projects, such as planning a birthday party for your best friend, or boring tasks like cleaning your room or organizing your closet. It works for building habits too, such as exercising regularly.

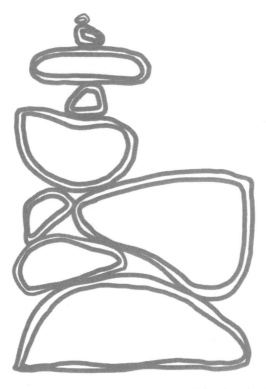

SCHEDULE TIME

If you're like most teens, you're stressed because you're busy: attending school, studying for tests, practicing your sport, writing college applications, and maybe working a part-time job. That's a lot to keep your eye on. Learning to schedule your time is a powerful skill to manage stress and feel more in control of your life. To schedule time, follow these steps:

1. Each day, schedule all your activities (homework, friend time, family time, after-school activities, and relaxation time).

2. Next to each task, write A, B, or C (where A is very important, B is moderately important, and C is not that important) to prioritize each task according to how important the task is to complete.

3. Schedule A-priority tasks in the earlier time slots (like 4:00 pm to 7:00 pm) in order to get the big things out of the way first. You'll worry less about running out of time once you've completed these.

4. Pay close attention to the period from 4:00 pm to 10:00 pm. This is crunch time, when you're trying to cram homework, relaxation, and friend and family time into a few hours in the evening. Planning and prioritizing during crunch time is particularly important.

⇆ *TRY IT HERE TOO:* Busy teens often don't prioritize sleep. They try to fit it in with all the other things they do. To sleep, it takes time to wind-down and relax. Scheduling your time will help you better manage your day and get the sleep you need. To sleep well takes planning, particularly when it comes to building in time to down-shift and prepare to sleep. When you schedule your day, schedule all your activities BUT schedule two sleep tasks for each day first: when you'll start your wind-down routine, and when you'll turn out the lights. These are priority A tasks. Once you've scheduled the sleep tasks, then schedule all the other things for the day around them. You'll learn more about skills to sleep better in Chapter 8: Health and Hormone Stress.

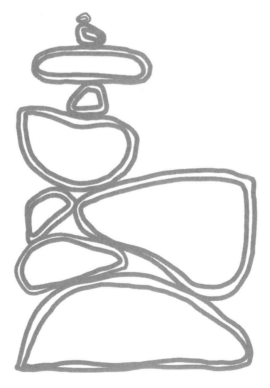

Estimate Time Accurately

Many people underestimate the time it takes to do something, and this creates a ton of stress. Underestimating the time a task takes means that you'll schedule too many tasks in the time you have. Work then piles up and your stress builds as you fall farther and farther behind. You miss deadlines, and you're always running a little late, whether it's turning in a paper, studying for a math test, or cleaning your room. But you can learn to estimate time accurately by following these steps:

1. Follow the steps from the previous activity and schedule all tasks.

2. Next to each task, write the amount of time you think the task will take.

3. As you complete each task, write the actual time it took to complete.

4. At the end of the day, rate how close you came to completing each task in the time that you scheduled for it (where 1 = bull's eye, 2 = close but no cigar, 3 = missed the target completely). Over time, you'll fine-tune your ability to estimate the amount of time tasks actually take. And as you get better at it, you'll finish more tasks in the time you have and you'll feel less stressed and overwhelmed in the process.

Check out Alesandro's *Estimate Time Accurately Exercise* for an example.

ALESANDRO'S ESTIMATE TIME ACCURATELY EXERCISE

Day of week: Tuesday   **Date:** March 8th

Time	Task	Estimated Time (mins.)	Actual Time (mins.)	Priority (A, B, C)	How Close? (1, 2, 3)
3:00 pm	End of school day				
4:00 pm	Band practice				
5:00 pm	Study for math test	30 mins.	50 mins.	A	3
6:00 pm	Dinner				
7:00 pm	History essay	60 mins.	95 mins.	B	3
8:00 pm	History essay	"	"	B	
9:00 pm	Watch my shows	60 mins.	70 mins.	C	2
10:00 pm	Wind down for sleep			A	
11:00 pm	Sleep				

-⚙- STRESS HACK: Here's a fun way to train yourself to estimate time accurately. As you go through your day, estimate what time it is. For example, on a Saturday, if you're out of bed at 11:00 am, estimate the time over the course of the day. Is it about 12:00 noon? Is it 3:00 pm? Check a clock or your phone for the time. How close were you to your estimate? With practice, your ability to estimate time accurately will improve.

-⚙- STRESS HACK: If you tend to underestimate how much time you'll take to complete a task, try doubling the time. If you guess you'll take 30 minutes to memorize the new vocabulary words for Spanish class, double the prediction to 60 minutes. If you think you'll take 60 minutes to write the History essay, set aside 120 minutes. Now, two hours is a lot of time to put into one task, so maybe break it down into four 30-minute study sessions and set an alert on your phone.

> 66 I started to feel more in control of my life once I started to schedule things and estimate accurately how much time each would take. It sounds simple, but I always came up with a reason not to schedule things I planned to do. Sometimes I told myself that I would remember everything. I didn't! Sometimes I convinced myself that I had plenty of time to do everything. I didn't! Sometimes, I told myself that I didn't even have time to schedule my day. I did! I'm glad I decided to try it. Not only am I feeling less stressed at the end of the day, but I'm getting more done during the day too.
> —Alesandro 99

Do It Now

People often procrastinate when they're stressed, but procrastinating tends to make things worse. These are the most common consequences of procrastinating:

- **When you procrastinate, your stress builds and builds.** Soon it feels like a huge mountain of stress that you have to climb in order to start. This causes you to procrastinate even more. So, you procrastinate to avoid stress, but you end up creating more stress.

- **When you procrastinate, you tend to produce lower-quality work when you finally get around to doing it.** Here's why. You're putting off starting a task but the clock is still ticking. At some point, you realize that you're running out of time and the fear of not finishing pushes you to start the task, but it's the 11th hour. You're nearly out of time. You rush to finish but you don't have enough time to do the task well. Then you feel terrible because the quality of the work isn't as good as it would have been if you had started the project earlier and stayed on it—and you know this. You might even get a poor grade because you rushed through the work.

- **When you procrastinate, you don't get enough sleep.** Night after night you put off starting work until very late. Now you're tired and having trouble concentrating. It's difficult to focus. You're making more mistakes, which creates more and more stress because the clock is ticking. You stay up later and later to finish your work. By the time you go to bed, your mind is racing, worrying, and stressing. Not a great formula for a good night of sleep.

- **When you procrastinate, your confidence takes a hit.** For example, if you're putting off studying for a test, you'll have less time to study. With less time to study you're less confident that you'll do well. Less confidence means more anxiety about the test. Now, on the day of the test, you're trying to do well on the test but feeling super anxious.

- **When you procrastinate, you can't fully enjoy the things you're doing while you're procrastinating.** For example, if you're watching your favorite shows or texting with friends rather than studying for that math test or writing that essay, these unfinished tasks hang over your head. Yes, you're watching your favorite show, but you're not enjoying it because you know that you're not working on homework and the clock is ticking.

If you procrastinate, you likely give yourself permission to put off starting tasks. You tell yourself that you'll do it later when you have more time, or more energy, or after you watch another YouTube video. You can learn to talk back to your *permission self-talk* and replace it with *do it now self-talk*. This can help you start and finish tasks so that you're less stressed and more successful. Follow these steps to do it now:

1. At the top of blank sheet of paper write a task you're putting off starting. Perhaps it's studying for a math final, or reading the last four pages of a chapter, or writing the first draft of an essay, or cleaning your room, or you name it.

2. Beneath the task, draw a line down the center of the page so that you have two columns. At the top of the left column, write *Permission to Procrastinate Self-Talk* and at the top of the right column, write *Do it Now Self-Talk*.

3. Close your eyes and see yourself starting the task but then stopping. Listen to the way you talked yourself into stopping. This is your *permission to procrastinate self-talk*. This self-talk doesn't play very loudly in your head but if you listen you'll hear it: "I'll do it after I text Jill," "I'll do it after I look up this one thing," "I'll do it after dinner," or, the all-time favorite, "I'll do it later." Write this *permission to procrastinate self-talk* in the left column of the page.

4. In the right column, write how you might talk yourself into starting the task. This is your *do it now self-talk*. To come up with ideas, imagine a friend who knows the truth about your procrastination and doesn't buy into the permission self-talk. This friend also knows the consequences you experience when you procrastinate. How would this friend—in a kind but firm way—talk to you to get you to start the task now. For example, to the permission self-talk, "I'll do it later," imagine your friend saying, "Really? How many times do you tell yourself, 'I'll do it later,' and you don't? Wouldn't you rather get this out of the way so you can enjoy watching your favorite show? Also, this math homework isn't easy. It will be a lot harder when you're tired. So, go ahead and do it now. Get it out of the way." To get an idea of how to do this, check the *Do It Now Self-Talk* that Deion came up with.

DEION'S PERMISSION TO PROCRASTINATE SELF-TALK AND DO IT NOW SELF-TALK

Permission to Procrastinate Self-Talk	Do It Now Self-Talk
It's okay. I'll do it later.	Yes, you'll do it later, maybe, but doing it later means that you'll be tired, and more stressed because you have less time to do it. Do it now.
This isn't a good time to start.	It's always a good time to knock something off your To Do list, especially when it only takes five minutes. Do it now so that you don't have to worry about it!
I'll do it later when I have more time.	The assignment is due tomorrow morning. Where will you find more time? You have six hours to do all your homework and putting this off only means that you'll be up late again. Do it now. Get it out of the way.
I need to think about this some more before I do it.	People solve problems and do things in steps. Why think more about something when you don't really know what you'll need to do after the first step? Start now and figure it out as you go along. Do it now.
I'll do it after I watch this episode.	Really? One episode tends to lead to the next. You know that. You're procrastinating. Watch the show after you finish your work. You'll enjoy it more without the unfinished work hanging over your head. Do it now.

I need to do more research before I start.	When does research become procrastination? You can do more research later after you have a better idea of where the project is headed. Also, don't confuse research with re-search. Just do a first pass and write down other things to research as you go along. Do it now.
I don't feel like doing it right now.	When will you feel like doing it? It's boring and it's hard. It won't get less boring or less hard by putting off starting it. Do it now so that you can move on to more interesting and easier things.
I'll do it when I have more energy.	If you're putting off starting then it probably means that it's hard. Yes, doing hard things takes energy but do you think you'll have more energy three hours later when you're tired, stressed, and want to sleep?

66   I never realized how often I talk myself into procrastinating. It's like a little birdie on my shoulder is giving me permission to put off things. It's the Do It Later birdie and it tweets, "Don't worry, you'll do it later," or, "You'll do it after you do this." When I listen to that birdie it feels okay to procrastinate. But I have a new little birdie on my other shoulder now. I call it the Do It Now birdie. I'm trying to listen to that birdie more often and it's working. The more I ignore the tweets of the Do It Later birdie and listen instead to the Do It Now birdie, the more I get done and the less stressed I feel.

—Deion 99

STRESS HACK: When you're stressed and putting off starting a task, it helps to think in terms of minutes rather than hours, or at least five minutes. A five-minute dash to the finish can help you start, and often starting is the hardest part. Here's how it works. Next time you're putting off working on that essay or reading that chapter, set the timer on your phone for five minutes. Anyone can work for five minutes, right? Now, try to complete as much work as you can in five minutes. After five minutes, set the timer for another five minutes. Now you've started . . . and it's easier to keep going! That's the five-minute dash.

Make Good Decisions Quickly

It's tough to get through the day without having to make some kind of decision. There are small decisions, of course: whether to watch a comedy or an action movie; whether to order the burger or the mac and cheese; whether to play the draw-two or the wild card in Uno. There are big decisions too, such as whether to share something personal with a friend or to keep it to yourself; whether to ask Jessie or Bobbi to the prom; or what colleges to apply to. Whether the decisions are small or big, simplifying decision-making can lessen the stress in your life. **ITEM** is a simple skill you can use to make decisions quickly:

- ***I*mportance of decision.** Not all decisions are of equal importance. The first step to make decisions quickly is to assign an importance to the decision. Some decisions are *small*, such as whether to go to the movies with a friend or not. Some decisions are *medium*, such as whether to prioritize studying for the math test or to finish the English essay that's due tomorrow. Still other decisions, although not as many as you think, are *big*, such as whether to attend a small or large college. The importance of the decision helps you decide how much time to spend making the decision.

- ***T*ime the decision.** If it's a *small* decision, give yourself 30 seconds to decide. For example, does it take more than 30 seconds to decide whether to have cereal or scrambled eggs for breakfast? If making small decisions like this tends to stress you out, remind yourself that small decisions have small consequences. You probably don't remember the small decisions you make every day, and there's a reason for that: they're small decisions! For *medium* decisions, take at most 30–60 minutes to decide. It helps to think through the pros and cons of the options you're considering. For *big* decisions, definitely think through the pros and cons of the options and run these by a friend or family member who you trust. For truly big decisions, it's okay to give yourself a couple of days or even weeks to think about the decision and speak to other people, but don't dwell on it too much. Even a big decision isn't likely to change your life forever, for better or for worse.

- ***E*liminate the perfect.** There's no such thing as the perfect decision. Every decision is the best decision of a set of possible decisions.

Some are less good than others, but no decision is the perfect decision that gives you the perfect result. People solve problems in steps. They make the first decision, observe what happened, and then make the second decision, and then the next. If you try to make the perfect decision, you're likely to fall into an analysis-paralysis trap because you can't know everything about everything, particularly before it happens.

- **Move on it.** Once you make a decision, move on it, even if moving on it means doing something small, such as making a to-do list for the day, or making the first call to someone. Moving on the decision means that you've finished deciding and planning and now you're acting.

STRESS HACK: Sometimes teens are told to start their homework with the most difficult and stressful task to get it out of the way. But starting your study period with the most difficult or stressful task can make you dread starting your homework in the first place. Not only that, depending on how stressed the task makes you feel, you might discover that it's not easy to stay on the task to finish it. At some point, you'll have to start the task you're dreading, but try to begin your homework with a task that builds your confidence and gets those mental gears engaged. Or, begin with a fun or pleasant task that lifts your mood a little. For example, if you like poetry and plan to include some in the essay you're writing, read the poems aloud to yourself or find your mom or dad and read the poems to them if they like poetry too. Plus, knowing you're going to accomplish something fun can make starting your homework a little more fun too. Once you're feeling a bit happy and confident, taking on that dreaded task is a little easier.

In a Nutshell

School and work stress is one of the biggest sources of stress for most teens. Deadlines, homework, job interviews, or just getting things done are challenges that every teen faces. Learning skills to deal with school and work stress will go a long way towards decreasing your stress in general.

CHAPTER 4
Performance and Test Stress

Pop quizzes, presentations, tests, and high-stakes exams like the SAT are a big part of teen stress. So are the practices, try-outs, playoffs, and big games if you're an athlete, and the recitals, auditions, and shows if you're a musician or actor. Everyone feels some degree of stress in situations like these, and some feel *very* stressed. Many of the skills in this chapter come from the field of performance psychology and can help you decrease your stress and improve your performance, whether it's for a test, a recital, or a playoff game. In this chapter, you'll learn the following inside and outside skills to deal with performance and test stress:

- Recover From Mistakes
- Focus to Finish
- Imagine Success
- Slip into the Present Moment
- Move Mindfully
- Reset Your Predict-o-meter
- Calculate Your Prediction Accuracy
- Surf the Panic Wave
- Coach Yourself to a Win
- Build Routines

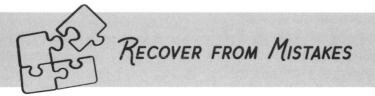

One of the biggest stresses in life is worrying about making mistakes. Worrying about dropping a pass. Worrying about forgetting an assignment. Worrying about missing a question on a test. But here's the thing. No matter how careful you are and how much you study and prepare, you're going to make mistakes. Even the smartest people and most skilled athletes and performers in the world regularly make mistakes. When it comes to excessive performance and test stress, the trick is to know how to bounce back when you make mistakes rather than trying to prevent them at all costs.

If you're like many stressed people, you put yourself down when you make a mistake. You might tell yourself that it's all your fault. You might

MISTAKE REPEAT CYCLE

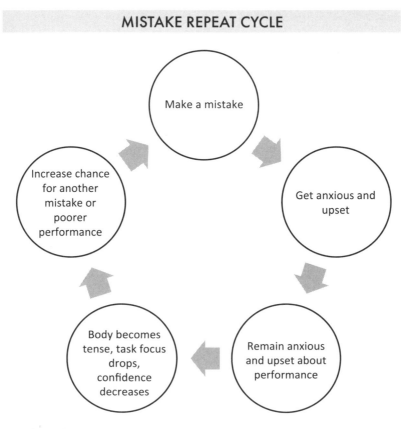

Make a mistake

Get anxious and upset

Remain anxious and upset about performance

Body becomes tense, task focus drops, confidence decreases

Increase chance for another mistake or poorer performance

call yourself names: idiot, loser, lazy. You might tell yourself that you can't do anything right. But beating yourself up in this way takes you away from your performance sweet spot: a body that is optimally tense and a mind that is optimally focused. Not only that, putting yourself down when you make a mistake lowers your confidence, which only increases the stress and anxiety you feel in your next performance or test. This is the Mistake Repeat Cycle.

But you can choose another path! In the Mistake Recovery Cycle, you see your mistake as just that: a mistake. You don't blame yourself but instead see it as an opportunity. A mistake means you're still in the game. You're still in the running for a win or a good grade. In this way, you remain confident, focused, and relaxed. Top-notch athletes, performers, and test-takers learn to recover from mistakes and do it quickly.

MISTAKE RECOVERY CYCLE

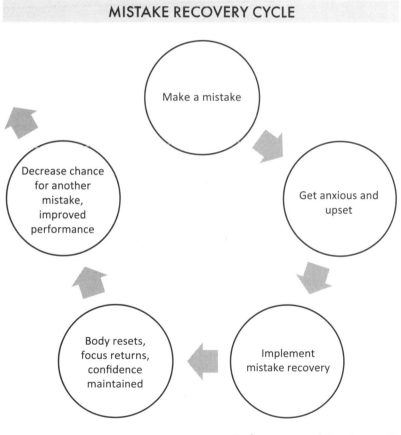

You've likely seen unhelpful mistake recovery plans. During a game you've seen a teammate blow up and scream at the referee or coach. During a test you've seen a student break a pencil and throw it across the room. And you've likely seen helpful mistake recovery plans in action too. That's the teammate who misses a shot, shakes it off, and makes the next one, or the friend who misses a note in her piano recital, recovers, and keeps playing. To develop your mistake recovery plan, follow these steps:

1. Use a physical signal to start mistake recovery. Physical signals anchor your mind and body. They're a great way to start mistake recovery, particularly in performances such as sports where you're focused on physical effort. For example, in tennis, walk across the back baseline a few feet. In soccer, pull up your socks. In other activities, you might close your eyes for a few seconds or open your eyes and count three clouds in the sky. In a test, you might open and close your hands three times, or put your pencil down and pick it up again. Whatever works for you!

2. Take three slow deep breaths to clear you head and re-center your body. If you can't take slow, deep breaths, just take a deep breath and blow it out forcefully.

3. Repeat a focus word or phrase to refocus on what's important: the next question on the test, or the ball that's still in play, the next note in your recital, or the next step in the ballet. If you're focusing on a word or phrase, you can't focus on the mistake. For example, "Move on," "Next shot," "Next question" are great re-focus phrases.

Take a look at the mistake recovery plans that Alesandro and Ofelia came up with and then take a few minutes and create your own mistake recovery plan.

ALESANDRO'S MISTAKE RECOVERY PLAN

Mistake: When I'm running and I make a bad pass.

Physical signal: Quick shake of my hands.

Breath: Deep breath in and quick forced breath out.

Focus word or phrase: Reset and go!

Mistake: When I miss an open shot.

Physical signal: Drop shoulders and rotate head.

Breath: Three deep slow breaths.

Focus word or phrase: Take your time. You're in charge now.

Mistake: When I don't get forward in time to receive a pass.

Physical signal: Quick shake of my hands.

Breath: Deep breath in and quick forced breath out.

Focus word or phrase: Reset and go!

OFELIA'S MISTAKE RECOVERY PLAN

Mistake: Don't understand question on test.

Physical signal: Put pencil down and pick it up again.

Breath: Deep breath in and quick forced breath out.

Focus word or phrase: Move on and come back.

Mistake: Don't know answer to question on test.

Physical signal: Put pencil down and pick it up again.

Breath: Deep breath in and quick forced breath out.

Focus word or phrase: Guess and move on.

⇆ TRY IT HERE TOO: You can develop a mistake recovery plan for any mistake, not just performance and test mistakes. You can make plans to recover from saying the wrong thing when hanging out with friends, or accidentally posting something on social media. The steps are the same.

☼ STRESS HACK: You can use imagery to turbo-charge mistake recovery. Write an imagery script in which you recover from a mistake quickly and perfectly. For example, you could write a script in which you're taking a test and you don't know how to answer the first few questions. You then imagine starting your recovering plan. You take three deep slow breaths, tap your pencil twice on the desk, then move to the next question while staying cool and confident. Then, imagine the answers to those first few questions popping into your head. You then return to the questions as you imagine writing the correct answers, then holding your head high with pride.

❝ I used to stress out before games—even practices—but I'm stressing less now after I created a mistake recovery plan. It really works! I'm playing better because I'm more relaxed. I'm even sleeping better before big games. I told my coach about mistake recovery and he asked me to teach it to my teammates. Now, everyone on the team has a mistake recovery plan and we're stressing less and playing better.

—Asif **❞**

Focus to Finish

Have you wondered how elite athletes, such as Simone Biles, or amazing musicians, such as Yo-Yo Ma, manage their stress during high-stakes performances? How do they stay calm when all eyes—hundreds or thousands or even millions of eyes—are on them, watching their every move? Well, it comes down to one word: focus. They're able to screen out all the unimportant things around them and focus on the most important thing in that moment: their performance. Focus is important in academics, too. In fact, whether you're on the field, on the stage, or in the classroom, your ability to focus is one of the most important skills you can develop to lessen stress and improve your chances of success.

Focus is the ability to tune out distractions and direct your full attention to the task at hand. The ability to focus during a performance or a practice, whether it's working on an algebra problem, pirouetting across the stage, or throwing a curve ball, has a big effect on how well you perform.

Here's how focus improves performance. The intensity of your focus is directly related to the arousal of your mind and body, which affects your muscle control, which affects your small and large motor skills. For example, if your mind is caught up in worrying about missing a shot on the court or

INFLUENCE OF POOR FOCUS ON PERFORMANCE

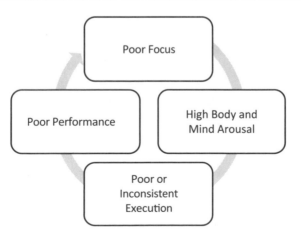

field, your body will feel tense. This tension or arousal affects how well you execute the shot. If you miss the shot, this sets you up to worry more about the next shot, which makes it even more difficult for you to focus.

On the other hand, if you're focused on only what's necessary to execute the task, then your body will follow that focus. For example, if at the free-throw line you focus only on "relax your body and release the ball" then your body and mind stay calm and relaxed and your body follows that focus. If your focus instead is on missing the shot, on losing the game, or on the shot you missed in the game last week, then you're less likely to make the shot in the moment.

INFLUENCE OF EFFECTIVE FOCUS ON PERFORMANCE

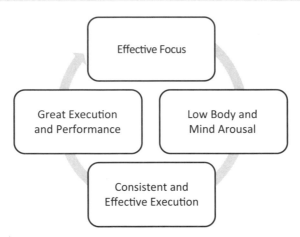

Learning to focus comes down to knowing what to focus on. When your mind is focused on the important and relevant things, your body responds in the ways it knows how to respond. These are the actions you've practiced repeatedly, day after day, hour after hour. Whether you've practiced algebra problems, or cross-field passes in soccer, or a particular piano piece, when you're focused on the action in the moment, your body will respond the way you've taught it to respond. All the things on which you could focus come down to two categories: relevant or irrelevant.

- **Relevant:** When you focus on things that are relevant, you're focusing on the things that have a direct influence on your performance. For example, if you pitch for your baseball team, then relevant points of focus are how you grip the baseball, which pitch

You remember what people said at a party or the song that was playing when you first met them. You learn by listening to your teacher or coach. You can remember the exact words people used when they spoke to you. You can identify a song by hearing the first few notes.

You remember physical details of situations and how your body feels as it executes an activity or skill. You can sit perfectly still and know what your muscles feel like when you make the perfect pass, or hit the perfect note, or turn the page of an exam booklet.

Include sounds in your images. For example, hear the swoosh of the basketball fall through the net; or the sound of your foot making solid contact with the ball; or each beautiful note as you play the clarinet; or the voice of your tutor as you take the exam saying, "Stay calm and centered."

Include the feel of muscle movements in your images. For example, feel the powerful push off the mat into a handspring; or the feel of the basketball curling off your fingertips as you shoot; or the easy relaxed feeling of your grip on the pencil or your fingers on the piano keys.

you select, and how you stand. In other words, the success of the pitch depends on those things that you have the most influence over.

- **Irrelevant:** When you focus on things that are irrelevant, you're focusing on the things that you have the least influence over, and therefore the least influence over your performance. For example, how well other people are doing on the math test is irrelevant to how well you do. Similarly, the number of people who watch your soccer match is irrelevant to how well you play. You'll still have to answer most of the math problems correctly to perform well on the test and you'll still have to kick and pass correctly to perform well in the game.

Now that you know what to focus on, the next step is to practice focusing on those things and not on irrelevant things. Performance always happens in the present moment, and the present moment is the single most important moment you have when it comes to performing well. If you're focused on the past or future, then you're focused on things that are irrelevant to how well you'll do in the moment at hand. To build your present-moment focus, find a quiet, comfortable place to practice, and follow these steps:

1. Select an object on which to focus. This can be a mark on a piece of paper, a spot on the wall, a ball, or another piece of sports equipment.

2. Stare at the object for 30 seconds. Think only about the object as you stare at it. If you're in the present moment, you're not thinking about the test you took last week, or the upcoming performance or game next week, or what you did in the morning or what you plan to do in the evening. You're just thinking about the object in front of you.

3. Gradually increase your practice time by five seconds each week, until you get up to a minute. With practice and a little time, your ability to focus will improve. Soon, you'll be able to focus to finish the pitch, the piano piece, or the math test.

> **STRESS HACK:** A simple way to keep your mind in the game is to write down all your non-performance concerns before a practice, a game, a show, or a test. For example, write down concerns about a sick pet, an argument with a friend, or the big essay that's due next week. Then, leave the list of concerns in your locker, car, or at home. Remind yourself that these concerns will be there after the practice, game, show, or test, and there's nothing to do about them now anyway. Afterward, you can focus fully on these concerns. It's not that these concerns are less important than the test or game you're in. They're likely far more important, but focusing on them during a performance will only increase your stress, impair your focus, and diminish your performance, which makes them unimportant in this moment.

> " I've heard that the difference between an athlete and a professional athlete is the pros know how to focus. But I thought you either had it or you didn't have it. I didn't know that you could learn to focus. Now that I've learned, I can see it works. During practice and games, I can zero in on what's important and push everything else to the sidelines. It works during tests too. I've even tried it during stressful conversations with my teachers. Focus is the difference that makes the difference!
> —Deion "

IMAGIN

If performance and tests stress y
a dropped shot, botched violin s
disaster, you can learn to imagin
the way elite athletes do. Throug
an experience in your mind, and
performance before you perform
prepare while lying in bed, sitting

Identify Your Imager Typ

Imagery uses all your senses—he
muscles (muscle memory)—to har
to achieve your goals, whether it's
You may lean toward one sense o
imager type will help you to get th
of imager types and identify the ty

IDENTIFY YO

If your imager type is . . .	Then .
Seeing	You remember the details of people You can remember you were wearing six months ago. Yo best by reading, an easily recall the col friend's eyes or hair or ask directions bas visual landmarks, "T the restaurant with th sign" or "My house i with white trim." Alth may not remember a name, you never forge

Hearing

Physical

Now that you know your imager type, it's time to practice. Imagery is like any skill—the more you practice imagery the better an imager you become. There are two steps to learning to imagine success:

- Paint vivid images.
- Paint successful images.

Paint Vivid Images

The clarity and vividness of the images you use makes a big difference in how well this skill works. At first, you might find that it's difficult to make your images vivid, but with practice you can boost the vividness of your images and their power. It's best to start by practicing with simple images and then increase the vividness and details as you practice more. Remember to include all your senses, and to emphasize images of your primary imagery type (seeing, hearing, or physical).

To practice painting vivid images, read the following description, and then close your eyes and see in your mind's eye the following image as vividly as possible:

Picture a lemon in the open palm of your hand. In your mind's eye, see the dimpled texture of the lemon. Adjust the color of the lemon in your mind until it's the exact color that you want to see. Pay attention to any marks on the skin of the lemon, the smooth surfaces, and rough surfaces. See the size of the lemon. Is it small or large? See yourself slicing the lemon and juice dripping from the cut pieces. Notice the smell of the lemon. Notice the texture of the lemon flesh, the pulp, the seeds. Is your mouth watering? Imagine the tart taste. See yourself squeezing the lemon and the juice running over your fingers. Is the juice warm or cool? Do you feel the sting of the acidic juice on your hand or the sticky feel?

Practice with the lemon image for 5 minutes three times each day. After each 5-minute practice, rate the vividness of the image, from 0 to 10 where 10 is the most vivid you can imagine. Keep practicing until the vividness is 8 or greater.

Paint Successful Images

Now that you can imagine vivid images, it's time to paint successful ones, too. To imagine success, it's essential that you see yourself executing skills (whether it's swinging a bat, drawing a bow across a violin string, or answering a math question on an exam) flawlessly. You want to see only success in your mind's eye.

Take a few minutes and write a script that describes the image in detail. Break down the particular skill into technical steps to see in your mind's eye. For example, if the skill is shooting a free throw, imagine standing with your feet shoulder-width apart, arms bent at the elbow, shoulders down and relaxed, eyes on the net, legs slightly bent at the knees, and so on. Once you have the script, close your eyes and see yourself executing the skill in detail, and don't forget to imagine the successful completion of the task (ball dropping through net, teammate catching cross-court pass, fingers striking keys smoothly, moving through test booklet quickly, etc.). Look at the script Asif developed for his long shot from the three-point line.

ASIF'S IMAGINE SUCCESS SCRIPT

I approach the three-point line from the left. My arms are relaxed at my hips. I feel the ball firm and comfortable in my hands. I push off the court with my right leg and pivot right to face the net. I feel calm and confident as I rise above the court. My eyes are on the net. Everything is quiet as I focus. I see a red laser line that arcs from me to the net. I raise my hands above my head. The ball is on my fingertips. My hands and arms shoot out powerfully as I watch the ball follow the red arc toward the net. I'm suspended in the air, watching the ball, in slow motion, moving toward the net. As I slowly drop to the court, I see the ball swoosh through the net. The other players move toward the ball and then away as I feel the court beneath my feet. I move into the action, my teammates nod at me and yell, "Great shot." I'm back in the flow of the game.

Once you have a script, set aside five minutes several times a day to practice. Rate the vividness of the image using that 0 to 10 scale and keep practicing until you can create clear, crisp, and vivid images. Mental training is the same as physical training. It doesn't matter whether you're practicing taking shots, playing the piano, or taking exams, regular and frequent practice is the key. Once you're able to create vivid images of you successfully executing a skill, practice imagining success before the performance (you can even arrive a few minutes early to do it), or after a practice. Did practice go the way you wanted? If yes, great! Imagine it again! If not, imagine what you could have done better. Imagine success during warm-up, between drills, and before a competition or test (the night before and in the bus or car on the way to the meet or to school). Imagining success helps rein in a stressed mind filled with "What if I fail?" "What if I screw up?" "What if we don't make the playoffs?"

Speak to your coaches, tutors, and teachers and ask if they would be willing to set aside the first ten minutes of a practice, a game, a tutoring session, or test to practice imagining success. It's an amazing experience to sit in a room of people all imagining success together.

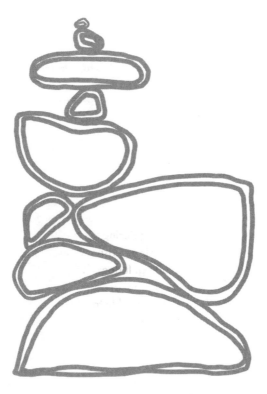

TRY IT HERE TOO: You can combine the imagining success skill with the mistake recovery skill you've learned. You can imagine making a mistake on an exam or during a practice or game, and then imagine recovering flawlessly and successfully. For example, you can imagine playing a wrong note and then imagine recovering quickly and flawlessly playing the rest of the song. You can imagine losing your cool during a game or on a test and then imagine pulling it together quickly. You can imagine that your energy level drops during the cross-country run and then imagine your energy level exploding as you race past everyone to cross the finish line.

STRESS HACK: Prior to the big game or recital, or even that big exam, write a newspaper or magazine headline of your success, "Sylvia Performs Bach Like a Master," or "Scouts are Eyeing Local Pitcher for the Big Leagues," or "Student Breaks School Record for Highest Score on Math Final," and then write the story of what happened as if it already did. This is a fun way to imagine success!

TRY IT HERE TOO: You can apply the imagine success skill in all types of situations. You can imagine successful conversations with teachers, friends, or parents. You can imagine successfully asking someone out, or confidently (head up, shoulders back, and smiling) interacting in an interview for a job or internship.

STRESS HACK: After you've written several imagine success scripts for different performance or test situations, read them aloud and record them. Then, create a playlist of these recordings and listen to them repeatedly. Also, listening to your playlist is a great way to practice imagining success during breaks in practice, and prior to and following tests, competitions, and performances.

> ❝ I have a very creative mind, which is cool, until I start to imagine the worst, like flunking a test, tripping over my words during a presentation, or going blank when someone I don't know well speaks to me. Over the last few months, I've been imagining success instead. I imagine doing well on my tests, giving interesting presentations, talking to new people AND keeping my cool while I do it. I've learned to use my creative mind to help me rather than to hold me back.
> —Lois ❞

Stress is often about spending time thinking about the future or about the past, and the antidote to this kind of stress is to spend time in the present moment. Slipping into the present moment means that you spend time observing the here and now, as it unfolds, in the moment.

Perhaps the easiest way to observe the present moment is to observe your breath. No matter where you go, there you are and there it is. Breathing mindfully invites feelings of peace and relaxation.

When you breathe mindfully, you attend to your breath without judgment. To attend to your breath in this way, anchor your attention on some part of your body that the breath touches. You might observe the feel of the air coming through your nose or mouth, or the rise and fall of your abdomen, or the way your ribs expand and contract with each breath in and out. Once you've anchored your attention to the breath, let go of each thought, each feeling, and each sensation that enters your awareness. You do this by acknowledging the thought, feeling, or sensation as it arises (perhaps saying gently to yourself, "thought" or "feeling" or "sensation") and then returning your attention to your breath. As you practice mindful breathing, you'll notice your attention wander away from your breath to greet thoughts—maybe even getting lost in them for a little while. Don't feel discouraged or frustrated by this. This is normal and natural. Our minds naturally distract us from what we're doing. Even people who have meditated for many years find that their minds wander. Perhaps through practice, you'll learn to rest your attention a bit more on your breath rather than on your thoughts, but you'll never be able to rid an unwanted thought from your mind or to lock your attention on your breath and keep it there. In fact, that's not the goal of mindfulness. The goal of mindfulness is not to eliminate or control your thoughts, but to change the way you relate to them. Instead of struggling with your thoughts, you learn to catch yourself when you're caught up in them, let go of them, and return to the present moment. In a sense, you learn to let go of pieces of your emotional responses, when they arise—as they inevitably will—and return to the present moment. Now try it. Here's a simple script to help you learn to anchor to the present moment through breathing mindfully. You can read it through first and then record yourself reading it and play it back—whatever works for you!

Close your eyes or fix your eyes on a spot in front of you and bring your attention to your breathing. Observe your breathing as if you've never encountered breathing before. Observe your breathing as if you're a curious scientist who wishes to observe the process closely without judgment. Notice the air as it enters your nostrils and goes down to the bottom of your lungs, and notice the air as it comes back out again. Notice how the air is slightly cooler as it goes in and slightly warmer as it goes out (pause for a count of 5). Notice the gentle rise and fall of your shoulders with each breath (pause for a count of 5) and the slow rise and fall of your rib cage (pause for a count of 5) and the comfortable rise and fall of your abdomen (pause for a count of 5). Rest your attention on one of these areas now, whichever you prefer, on the breath moving in and out of your nostrils, on the gentle rise and fall of your shoulders, or the easy rise and fall of your abdomen. Rest your attention on this spot now and notice the in and out of the breath (pause for a count of 10).

Whatever feelings, urges, or sensations come up, whether pleasant or unpleasant, gently acknowledge them as if nodding your head at someone passing by you on the street, and return your attention to the breath (pause for a count of 10). Whatever thoughts, images, or memories arise, whether comfortable or uncomfortable, gently acknowledge them and let them be. Let them come and go as they please and return your attention to the breath (pause for a count of 10). No matter how often you drift off into your thoughts, whether a hundred times or a thousand, simply note what distracted you and return your attention to the breath (pause for a count of 10). Again and again, your mind will wander away from the breath. This is normal and natural and happens to everyone. Our minds naturally distract us from what we're doing, so each time this happens, gently acknowledge it, notice what distracted you, and then return you attention to the breath (pause for a count of 10). If stress, anxiety, frustration, boredom, or other feelings arise, simply acknowledge them, and return your attention to the breath (pause for a count of 10). No matter how often your mind wanders, gently acknowledge it, note what distracted you, and return your attention to the breath (pause for a count of 10).

Practice breathing mindfully three times a day. Start with just two minutes of practice each time and add a minute every few days as you become more comfortable and confident, up to five minutes. Once you reach five minutes per practice, try bundling these five-minute practices into a single 15-minute practice. The benefits of these longer periods of mindful breathing can last for many hours, which make it well worth the time you set aside to do it. To help you remember to practice, link it to something you do every day—for example, before you shower, before you eat, or before you brush your teeth.

TRY IT HERE TOO: Since your breath goes where you go, you can slip into the present moment at *any* time. Try breathing mindfully for a few minutes before a test or a competition. Try breathing mindfully before a difficult conversation with a friend or teacher or before an interview for a job. In fact, try breathing mindfully at bedtime. It's a great way to prepare your mind and body for sleep.

STRESS HACK: You're a busy teenager, so it's not easy to remember to take a present-moment break, much less find 15 minutes to do it. Hitting the present moment reset button is an easy way to remember to take a quick present-moment break. Here's how to do it. On six or eight sticky notes, draw a dime-size circle in the middle. Color in the circle so that it looks like a button. Now, place a sticky note where you want to reset to the preset moment. For example, place one near the light switch in your bedroom, and one near the light switch on the front door. Place one on the back of your phone, or on the cover of your notebook, or on the corner of your desk. When you want to reset to the present moment, press the button on the sticky note. Then, anchor to your senses: what do you see, what do you hear, what do you feel, what do you taste? For example, when you hit the present-moment reset button on your desk in class, feel the chair pressed against your back, hear the other people talking, smell the fragrance of the perfume the girl seated next to you is wearing, taste the mint flavor of the toothpaste you used that morning. Having the visual reminders to take a reset can really help!

MOVE MINDFULLY

If you're an active person, another easy way to de-stress is to move mindfully. This means that a physical activity—such as walking, dancing, or even taking a shower—is your present-moment anchor, rather than your breath. Anchoring to physical activities enables you to observe every detail of the experience of a physical activity. It doesn't matter what activity you choose, so long as it's brief, you can do it every day, and you can use all your senses as you do it (smell, see, touch, hear, taste). For example, as you walk from the kitchen to the front door, focus on the smell of your house. See the pattern in the carpet or drapes. Feel the weight beneath your feet and the sound you make walking across the carpet or floor. Hear the sound your backpack makes as you pick it up and throw it over your shoulder. Taste the flavor of the banana you ate for breakfast.

As you practice mindfulness during these activities, observe any thoughts that enter your mind. Notice them, then return your attention to the sensory details of the activity. As your attention drifts away, gently nudge it back to the sensory details of what you're doing in that moment.

You might want to use signs or signals to remind yourself to act mindfully. If you plan to eat breakfast mindfully, make a paper placemat on which you've written "mindful." If you plan to walk up the stairs mindfully, place a sign on the step to remind you. If you wish to practice walking mindfully home, pick a house or store front along the way that's your "mindful" spot to remind yourself to shift your attention to mindful walking.

Over the next few days, try anchoring to activities. You might want to begin with just a single daily activity and practice it for a week. Later, add another activity and another. Try to plan activities throughout the day so that you're practicing mindful activities all day long.

MOVE-MINDFULLY ACTIVITIES

Showering	Washing Hands	Brushing Teeth	Combing Hair
Cooking	Spreading Jam	Eating	Drinking
Running	Walking	Dancing	Climbing Stairs
Writing	Texting	Typing	Drawing
Molding Clay	Knitting	Sewing	Painting
Stretching	Applying Lotion	Painting Nails	Applying Makeup
Playing Guitar	Humming	Singing	Reading Aloud
Folding Clothes	Washing Dishes	Drying Dishes	Making Bed

❝ I like the mindfulness of the breath meditation, but sometimes I'm so stressed out I don't take the time to do it. That's when I try moving mindfully. I do this during tests and when I'm on the field for a game or practice. In a test, I mindfully move my finger along the words as I read the question. In a game, I mindfully run onto the field or mindfully chew gum when I'm watching the game from the bench. I've even tried moving mindfully when I'm walking between classes to give me a few minutes in the present moment. It's a great stress buster.

—Alesandro **❞**

RESET YOUR PREDICT-O-METER

Often, what is or isn't stressful depends on your tendency to predict events in a certain way. We all do this and therefore, we all have a predict-o-meter. However, the problem isn't that you have a predict-o-meter, but that it repeatedly predicts inaccurately, and then you feel unnecessarily anxious and stressed. You likely are not even aware of this tendency to make inaccurate predictions. In fact, you might not even stop to ask yourself two important questions: "What is the prediction I'm making?" and "How likely is it that this prediction is true?"

To reset your predict-o-meter, you'll track not only your predictions but also the accuracy of those predictions. Sometimes simply realizing the amount your predict-o-meter is out of whack is enough to lower your stress. On a blank sheet of paper, create a Prediction Log. Look at the one Kanesha created to see how it's done. For the next two weeks, every time you predict a negative outcome, such as failing a test or losing a soccer match, record the prediction and indicate how strongly you believe the prediction is true (0 to 100%, where 100% means that you believe the prediction is completely true or accurate) and what really happened. If your prediction is false, place a check mark by it.

Look at Kanesha's predictions log. For a week, Kanesha wrote all of her worst-case predictions about failing a test, about her coach benching her, a friend dumping her, and about her boss firing her. Of the five anxious predictions that Kanesha made, only one came true: she got a bad grade on a math quiz because she had to study all night for a big history test.

KANESHA'S PREDICTION LOG

What negative thing will happen and when?	Strength of Your Belief (0–100%)	What really happened?	Check False Predictions (√)
I've studied all night and I'm still going to fail the history test.	85%	I got a B- on the test. That's not failing	√
Coach is never going to let me play again because I missed a game.	100%	Coach understood I had a family commitment and still started me in the next game.	√
Anya didn't return my texts because she doesn't want to hang out with me anymore.	90%	Anya lost her phone and things were fine once we connected.	√
My boss will fire me because I was 10 minutes late.	80%	She asked me to try not to be late again, smiled at me. She didn't fire me.	√
I'll get a bad grade on the math quiz tomorrow.	90%	I got a D+ because I didn't have time to study for it because I was studying for the history test.	

-💡- *STRESS HACK:* Self-hypnosis is a great way to relax when you're facing a stressful problem or challenge, and this is an easy self-hypnosis exercise. Set aside 30 minutes and sit in a comfortable chair in a quiet room. Now, consider an upcoming stressful challenge, such as doing well on an upcoming test. Next, select a phrase that is the opposite of what you're worried might happen. For example, *I'll do okay on the test. Now, relax.* Next, take several deep breaths and touch your thumb to your index finger while you remember a relaxing moment (for example, after a long run or lying on the beach in the sunshine). Then, say the phrase softly to yourself. Next, take several deep breaths and touch your thumb to your middle finger as you remember a loving moment (for example, a hug from your best friend or your pet snuggling in your lap). Then, say the phrase softly to yourself again. Next, take several deep breaths and touch your thumb to your ring finger as you remember accepting the nicest compliment you've ever received. Then, say the phrase softly to yourself again. Next, take several deep breaths and touch your thumb to your little finger as you remember the most beautiful place you've ever been. Then, say the phrase softly to yourself one last time. Finish by resting in this beautiful place for several minutes.

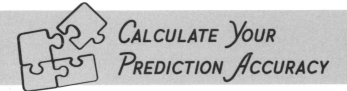
Another way to lessen your stress is to calculate the true accuracy of your predictions. To do this, follow these steps:

1. Think back over the last month and write down on a piece of paper a specific negative prediction (for example, "My boyfriend will dump me," or "I'll fail the test tomorrow," or "My friends will never invite me to hang out with them.").

2. Estimate the total number of times you made this negative prediction in the past month and write this number on the piece of paper.

3. Estimate the number of times this prediction came *true* in the last month and write this number on the piece of paper.

4. Now, divide the number of times that the prediction came true by the total number of times you made this prediction. This is your Prediction Accuracy. You can calculate your Prediction Accuracy for all the negative predictions you make about all kinds of things.

Look at Kanesha's Prediction Accuracy calculations. She calculated the accuracy of her prediction over the last month that all her friends won't want to hang out with her anymore (for no reason).

KANESHA'S PREDICTION ACCURACY CALCULATION

Prediction: My friends are going to leave me.	
Q1: How many times have you made this prediction in the past month?	90
Q2: How many times in the past month has this prediction come true?	0
Validity Quotient (Q2/Q1) × 100%	0%

Kanesha never stopped to consider the accuracy of her predictions. Each prediction seemed very true to her at the time. From then on, Kanesha calculated the accuracy of the negative predictions that she repeatedly made.

-☼- *STRESS HACK:* When you're stressed, your mind tends to drift toward doom and gloom. You can train your mind to tilt toward the positive—or at least toward the neutral—by looking for and spending time with the positive. It's not that you're making a negative into a positive. Instead, tilting toward the positive means seeing the positive that's there, no matter how small the positive may be. The positive can be a hummingbird in flight, a kind word from a friend, or accomplishing a goal. Each day, look for a positive moment and stay with it for 5 to 10 seconds. Open yourself to the positive experience. Let it fill your mind and body. Imagine the positive experience as a warm glow spreading through your chest and settling deep inside you. For example, watch the hummingbird bounce up and down in the air and allow the wonder and joy to fill you for a few seconds. Just a few seconds of taking in the positive every day links one positive moment to another to create a buffer of positive experiences that can insulate you from the stress of the day.

66 I had no idea how out of whack my predictions are and how much these inaccurate predictions increase my stress. Once I understood this, I started to doubt my predictions. This helped a lot. Now I'm much less likely to just go with my predictions and more likely to ask myself, "How likely is this to happen?"
—Kanesha **99**

-🔆- *STRESS HACK:* Tracking your anxious predictions is an easy way to correct your mind's tendency to overestimate the likelihood of bad things happening. Here are a couple of fun ways to do it. Fill your *right* pocket with 10 pennies, or Tic Tac candies, or paper clips, or other small items. During the day, each time you predict something bad might happen *and it comes true*, move one of the pennies or paper clips to the *left* pocket. Or, take two boxes of Tic Tac candies in different colors (for example, white and blue). Each time you make an anxious prediction, eat a white Tic Tac from the box. If the anxious prediction comes true, then eat a blue Tic Tac. At the end of the day, check the number pennies or paper clips in your left pocket, or the number of Tic Tac candies in each box.

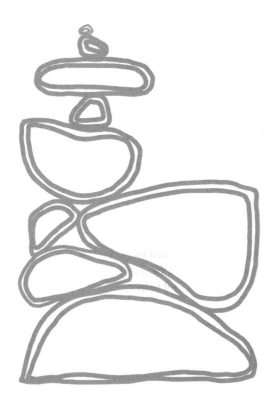

Surf the Panic Wave

Sometimes performance and test stress (or any kind of stress) builds and builds until you're flooded with panic. A panic attack is a sudden rush of fear or terror that includes intense physical sensations. These intense physical sensations are your body's alarm system sounding danger. Your heart might beat very fast, you might sweat, feel dizzy, and have trouble breathing. You might feel like you're choking, or your body might shake and tremble. Your mind sounds an alarm, too. If there isn't a *real and immediate* danger when you're having these intense bodily fear sensations, your mind will jump to reasons that seem to make sense at the time. You might think that you're going crazy, or dying, or that you're going to lose control and do something crazy, like running around and screaming at the top of your lungs.

In other words, a panic attack is your fear response. When you have a panic attack, your body and mind are sounding your fear alarm that something dangerous is happening to you, but nothing dangerous is happening or will happen That's why a panic attack is a false alarm.

Although you might believe panic attacks come out of nowhere, they really build like a wave. As the panic wave builds, you feel more and more panicky as you worry that you're headed for something dangerous. That's when you start to fight the panicky feelings. Fighting panicky feelings doesn't work. Just like an ocean wave, the panic wave is too strong. As you push against the building panic wave, you realize that you can't stop it, and as you realize this you feel more and more out of control of your mind and body until—boom—the wave peaks and you panic. After a few minutes, the wave begins to break as the panic attack ends, but the cycle begins again when you worry about the next one. In other words, fighting panicky feelings is 90% of the problem.

Therefore, it's really important not to fight the beginnings of the panic wave. Instead, it's better to surf the wave while you wait for it to die out. A Surf the Panic Wave plan will help with that, and it includes three parts:

- First Signs of the Panic Wave

- Jump Back from Panic Self-Talk

- Surf the Panic Wave Self-Talk

First Signs of the Panic Wave

The first part of the Surf the Panic Wave Plan is to identify the first signs that the panic wave is building. Different people have different panic wave signs with different intensities, but most people feel something. Some feel queasy or like they're going to throw up when they're nervous. Others feel like they're having trouble breathing or feel a little dizzy or lightheaded. Others feel their heart beating very fast or their hands and legs trembling. It's a mistake to ignore the first signs of the building wave and hope that the wave will go away. While you don't want to fight the wave, you don't want to ignore it either.

Look at the list of typical first signs of the panic wave. On a blank sheet of paper, write first signs you feel when a panic waving is coming. Rate how afraid you are of the sign, from 0 to 10 (where 0 is no fear and 10 is extreme fear). Write the fear number next to each panic wave sign.

TYPICAL FIRST SIGNS OF THE PANIC WAVE

Chest discomfort	Dizzy, lightheaded, or faint
Sweating	Shaking or trembling
Heart beating faster	Chills or flushing
Nausea or butterflies in stomach	Numbness or tingling
Shortness of breath	Choking feelings, difficulty swallowing
Feeling like you're not fully present	Feeling detached from surroundings

Jump Back from Panic Self-Talk

The second part of the Surf the Panic Wave Plan includes jumping back from panic self-talk. You'll use jump back talk to remind yourself that your panicky feelings (the first signs of panic) aren't dangerous. Replacing your *jump to panic self-talk* with *jump back from panic self-talk* makes it easier to surf the panic wave. It's always easier to hang out with scary or uncomfortable feelings if you believe, even a little, that they aren't dangerous. Look at the list of Jump Back from Panic Self-Talk and include the self-talk that fits for you in your plan.

Jump To Panic Self-Talk	Jump Back from Panic Self-Talk
I'm having a heart attack.	I'm not having a heart attack. My heart is beating fast because I'm scared. My heart is young and healthy. It can take a lot. If I was running track and my heart was beating this fast, I wouldn't feel scared. Moving around calms me and doesn't hurt like it would if I was having a heart attack.
I'm going to faint or pass out.	I feel dizzy because a little less blood is flowing to my brain. This is normal when you're scared and doesn't mean that I'm going to faint. I won't faint when I'm scared because when I'm scared my blood pressure is high, not low (and low blood pressure is what causes most people to faint).
I'm suffocating.	This feeling isn't dangerous. I'm not going to suffocate. I'm feeling short of breath because my neck and chest muscles are tight. That happens when I'm scared. I'm getting plenty of oxygen. It just feels like I'm not. My body knows how to take care of me. My body knows how to breathe.
I'm paralyzed or going to fall.	My legs are weak or shaking because I'm scared. I'm not going to fall just because I'm scared. My legs are strong. If I really need to walk or run, my body can do this because that's what my body would do if I was in real danger.

I'm going crazy.	I feel strange because I'm scared. My body is out of control because I'm scared but this doesn't mean I'm crazy. This feeling is unpleasant but it isn't dangerous.
	A panic attack is the fear response. If I was feeling this way and there was a real danger, I wouldn't think I was going crazy. I'd think I was scared.
I'm losing control.	Feeling like I want to get up and run doesn't mean I'm losing control. It's natural to want to get up and move around when you're scared.
	Even if I did scream and run away, that doesn't mean I've lost control. I might run away if something truly dangerous happened. It's my body's way of protecting me.

Surf the Panic Wave Self-Talk

The third and final part of the Surf the Panic Wave Plan includes Surf the Panic Wave Self-Talk. This is a calm mind skill. It's much easier to surf the panic wave when you believe you can do it. Surf the Panic Wave Self-Talk is a pep talk that you give yourself. It's a way to calm yourself in a supportive way. Surf the Panic Wave Self-Talk helps you to accept the feelings, surf the panic wave, and remain patient while you wait for the wave to pass. Look at the list of Surf the Panic Wave Self-Talk and include the ones you like in your Surf the Panic Wave Plan.

SURF THE PANIC WAVE SELF-TALK

These panicky feelings are a wave. They come and go. I'll just surf them, up and down.

These feelings come and go like a wave. The wave weakens and decreases over time. All I have to do is surf the wave.

I'm going to surf these panicky feelings and wait for them to pass.

I can handle these feelings. They aren't dangerous.

These feelings are uncomfortable, but I can handle them.

I've surfed this wave before. I can do it again.

I can feel anxious and still handle these feelings.

I'll just let my body do its thing. This will pass.

It's okay to feel anxious. It's okay to surf the wave. It's okay to just be.

I've surfed on this wave before. I can do it again.

I'm getting good at surfing the panic wave. I'm a first-rate surfer.

This feeling isn't dangerous. Nothing is wrong.

Fighting the panic wave doesn't help. It just makes it worse. Surfing the wave is the only thing to do.

These feelings won't hurt me, even though it doesn't feel good.

These worries aren't real. They're just thoughts and I'm not in danger.

Nothing serious is going to happen to me. It never has before. I'm anxious, uncomfortable, and okay.

This is just anxiety. I'm not in danger. I'll just let these feelings pass.

Create a Surf the Panic Wave Plan

Now it's time to put the parts together to create your Surf the Panic Wave Plan. Although it isn't easy to surf the panic wave, it's a bit easier when you have a plan. On a blank sheet of paper, write the three parts of your plan: *First Signs of the Panic Wave; Jump Back from Panic Self-Talk; Surf the Panic Wave Self-Talk.* Then add a fourth section for some of your favorite calm body skills. Then in each part write the skills and important things you want to remember when you begin to feel the panic wave building. To get an idea how to do this, look at Asif's *Surf the Panic Wave Plan.* Once you've created your plan, put it somewhere where you can find it quickly when you feel the panic wave coming on.

ASIF'S SURF THE PANIC WAVE PLAN
Don't Fight the Wave, Surf It

My First Signs of Panic	The first sign of the panic wave is when I start to have trouble breathing. I'm afraid that I'm going to suffocate or to stop breathing and die.
My Favorite Jump Backs from Panic	This feeling isn't dangerous. I'm not going to suffocate. I'm feeling short of breath because my neck and chest muscles are tight. That happens when I'm scared. I'm getting plenty of oxygen. It just feels like I'm not. My body knows how to take care of me. My body knows how to breathe.
My Favorite Surf the Wave Self-Talk	These panicky feelings are a wave. They come and go. I'll just surf them, up and down. These feelings come and go like a wave. The wave weakens and decreases over time. All I have to do is surf the wave. Surf the wave. I've surfed this wave before. I can do it again. Nothing serious is going to happen to me. It never has before. I'm anxious and okay.
My Favorite Calm Body Skills	I'll breathe slowly and deeply. I'll relax and refresh.

One last word about surfing the panic wave: Just like a real wave, a panic wave rises and falls. When you first use your surf the panic wave plan, you'll see that it works. The panic wave starts to fall. You might then think you're out of the woods. The panicky feelings are gone for good or for at least that day. However, it's important to remember that although the panic wave falls, it can (and will) rise again. That's why it's a wave. It rises and falls. Sometimes people become alarmed when the panic wave rises again after the first panicky feelings decrease. Don't be alarmed. Surf the wave as it rises and falls. Over time, the intensity of the panic wave diminishes, just like a real wave.

> **"** I was in math class when the first panic attack hit. My heart started to pound, I felt dizzy, and my arms and hands tingled. I thought I was dying. I went to the school nurse who told me I had a panic attack and that although panic attacks are very scary, they aren't dangerous. That helped, but I still worried when I had these panicky feelings. Then I learned how to surf the panic wave. At first, I was scared when the panicky feelings started to build, but it didn't take long for me to learn to ride it out. Now, I hardly think about the panicky feelings, and when I do, I don't worry because I know how to surf them and that helps a lot!
>
> —Asif **"**

-⚙️- *STRESS HACK:* A quick way to calm down when you feel panicky is to take the cold-water plunge. Cold water activates the vagus nerve, which triggers the calming branch of your autonomic (or automatic) nervous system. The autonomic nervous system controls things you don't have to think about, like your breathing or your heart beating. Next time you're feeling super stressed, take a shower and finish with 30 seconds of cold water. Or submerge your face in a big bowl of ice-cold water. I know, it sounds weird! But it works. You'll feel more relaxed afterward. Also, you can strengthen your calming response with regular cold-water practice. After each shower, extend the time you stand in cold water. Start with 15 seconds and over time work your way up to longer periods of time.

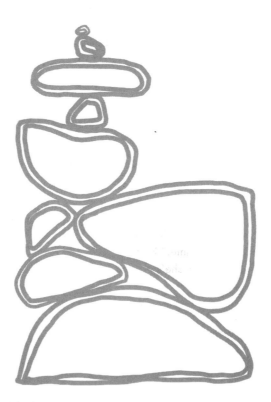

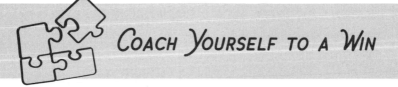

Coach Yourself to a Win

Have you ever had a coach that stresses you out? Of course you have. Coaches can either stress you out or calm you down. They can encourage you or criticize you. They can build your confidence or tear it down. But whether you have a good coach or a bad coach, the most important coach is the one that lives in your head. This is called self-talk. Sometimes the self-talk is helpful: "I can do this," "That was a great pass I made," "I'm smart and doing okay on this test." Sometimes, though, the self-talk is unhelpful: "I can't do this," "I can't pass the ball to save my life," "I'm stupid and going to flunk this test." What you say to yourself is powerful. The good news is that you have control over what you say to yourself, which means that you can harness the power of your coaching self-talk to lower your stress and improve your performance in all areas of your life.

Helpful self-talk creates emotions that enhance your performance and unhelpful self-talk creates emotions that undermine it. That's because emotions have physical consequences, such as your heart and breathing rate, your muscle tension, and your ability to concentrate and focus. For example, Bob and Beth are taking a test. Bob's coaching self-talk is unhelpful. He's thinking, "I can't believe I don't know the answer to this question. I'm an idiot. I should have known this material would be on the test. Now I'm going to fail the test and the whole class." Bob is stressed and angry. His body is tight, he's having trouble focusing. He's having trouble remembering what he studied and knew before he sat down in his chair. Bob may not do well on the test, but not because he isn't smart and well prepared. Bob may fail the test because of the way he's talking to himself. Beth is taking the same test. She's as smart and as prepared as Bob, but her coaching self-talk is helpful. She's thinking, "Relax. You studied and you're smart. Take one question at a time." Beth is focused and calm and as she works her way through the test, she's growing more confident that she's on top of it.

POSITIVE AND NEGATIVE COACHING SELF-TALK

Positive Coaching Self-Talk	Emotional Consequence	Physical Consequence
"I finished. It was worth it."	Relief	Relaxed body, good focus
"I'm going for it."	Determination	Relaxed body, good focus
"I can do this."	Excitement	Relaxed body, good focus
"I'm doing fine."	Relaxation	Relaxed body, good focus

Negative Coaching Self-Talk	Emotional Consequence	Physical Consequence
"What if I blow it?"	Worry and stress	Tense body, poor focus
"I always screw up."	Frustration	Tense body, poor focus
"Losing isn't an option."	Anxiety and stress	Tense body, poor focus
"I let my team down again."	Sadness	Tense body, poor focus

There are two steps to learning to coach yourself to win. The first step is to learn to pay attention to the way you talk to yourself. Self-talk happens quickly and often under the radar, but you can become more aware of it by tracking your self-talk patterns. The next time you feel yourself getting stressed about a performance, take a moment to stop and pay attention to your self-talk. What messages are you sending yourself? Here are two other ways to identify your coaching self-talk:

- **Revisit past performances:** Think back to your successful and unsuccessful performances, athletic or academic. Try to remember what was going through your mind and how you felt. Don't worry if you can't remember exactly what you were thinking or feeling. Just jot down what you do remember and look for patterns.

- **Visit current performances:** Before and after every practice, game, study session, or test, identify your self-talk patterns and how they affected your performance. Try to do this as soon as you can when you're more likely to remember exactly what you were thinking and feeling.

Write these thoughts in a small notebook and keep the notebook in your book bag or locker. Or you can write in your phone note app. At first, you may have trouble identifying your self-talk. Just keep at it. After a few days it gets easier.

Now that you've identified your coaching self-talk patterns, the second step is to learn to change your unhelpful coaching self-talk into helpful self-talk. There are three ways to do this:

- **Countering:** When you notice that you're talking to yourself in unhelpful ways, try countering it with more reasonable and calming thoughts. This is particularly true when you slip into one of those thinking traps you learned in Chapter 3. For example, to the unhelpful self-talk, "I'll never make the team," counter this thought by asking yourself reasonable questions such as, "Why wouldn't I make the team? What makes me think that I'll never make the team? What makes me think that I *might* make the team?"

- **Reframing:** Reframing means you look at a situation but from a different and more positive point of view. It's like putting a so-so painting in a beautiful frame. Although it's still not a masterpiece, it does look a whole lot better. It's the same with self-talk. You can take a situation that looks negative at first and reframe it in a less negative or dreadful way. For example, let's say you're having trouble making solid passes to your teammates during a basketball game. Your unhelpful coaching self-talk might sound like, "I can't do this. All my passes suck! I've tried everything and nothing works." You can reframe the situation by saying to yourself, "I'm not making solid passes yet, but it's early in the game, and I can get better. It always takes me a little while to get in the groove, but I always get there."

- **Affirming:** Affirming means that you focus on the positive and keep your focus there. The first step is to write out positive affirmations about your performance. Effective affirmations help you feel better and focus on the good. Write the affirmations in the present tense ("I am," instead of "I will."). Try to be as specific as you can ("swing through the ball," instead of "play a good round of golf today."). Last, make the affirmation positive rather than NOT negative ("relaxed," instead of "not nervous."). Check out some affirmations for a kid playing during a piano recital and another who is on the swim team:

I'm floating in the music. I have a nice touch on the keyboard. I'm confident and prepared. I'll play from my heart. I'll hit every note and then move on. I'll ride the wave of the music with a clear and focused mind as every note sounds smooth and clear beneath my fingertips.

I'm the hardest working swimmer on the 100-meter relay team. I've got fire in my belly that makes me work harder and smarter. On the block, I feel the fire but I feel calm too because I'm prepared and ready.

After you've written your affirmations, spend a few minutes each day reading through them. Practice saying the affirmations to yourself, almost like a meditation.

STRESS HACK: When you're coaching yourself, the tone of your coaching self-talk is as important as the words you use. A harsh, critical tone, even with encouraging words, can increase your stress and hurt your performance. To see how this works, stand in front of a mirror, look at yourself, scowl, and yell "Relax!" How does that feel? Then, look in the mirror, smile, and in a soft, soothing voice, say "Relax." How did that feel? To be the coach you want to be to yourself, practice your coaching self-talk in front of a mirror. Start by speaking to yourself at a normal volume with a relaxed, soothing, and confident look on your face. After a minute or two, switch to whispering the coaching self-talk to yourself with that same relaxed, soothing, and confident look. Last, switch to just thinking the coaching self-talk as you look at yourself in the mirror with that relaxed and confident look. Practice this every day, and particularly before a practice or game, a quiz or test, or any performance.

66 I've had good coaches and I've had bad coaches, but I never thought about the coach in my head. Once I started to pay attention to him, I didn't like him. He was worse than the worst coach I've ever had. Once I realized that, I decided to change my coaching style. Now, I'm less hard on myself. When I coach myself, I'm encouraging rather than critical and it's paying off. I'm way less stressed before games, and I'm playing better too.
—Alesandro 99

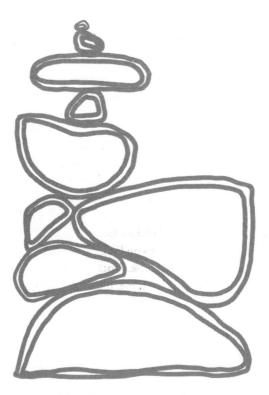

BUILD ROUTINES

Chaos is stressful and routines change chaos into predictability. A routine is a planned and predictable course of action that improves your focus so that you can perform well in both practice and the performance, regardless of the kind of performance it is. Whether you're performing in a sport, in a test, or in a musical recital or play, routines help you to build habits, and habits help you to stop thinking and just perform, letting your body and mind do what you've practiced and trained them to do.

Imagine a funnel with a ball in it. The funnel represents your routines and the ball represents your focus. At the top of the funnel is your pre-performance routine. In this part of the funnel, you focus is open and includes the thoughts and actions that you use to get ready for the performance (whether the performance is a practice or the real deal). For example, let's say you're playing a violin recital. Your pre-performance routine might include showing up at the auditorium an hour before the recital, stretching your arms and fingers for 10 minutes while you listen to a particular playlist that's relaxing. As the recital gets closer, the ball moves farther down the funnel as your focus narrows. You engage in other routines, such as tuning your violin, playing several scales, and perhaps closing your eyes and imagining a positive and successful performance. These routines eliminate distractions and direct your attention to preparing and performing. Finally, the ball enters the bottom of the funnel. Here your focus narrows even more. These routines are the few minutes before the practice or performance itself. You stand in the wings of the stage, take several slow deep breaths, and hum the song you'll play.

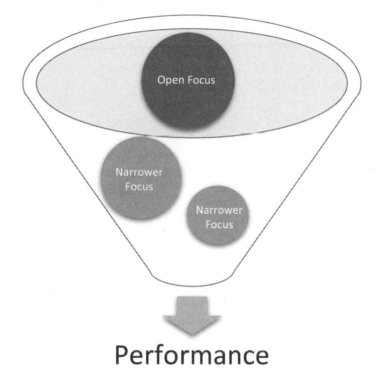

FUNNEL OF FOCUS

Open Focus

Narrower Focus

Narrower Focus

Performance

Routines don't guarantee that you won't lose your focus during a performance or practice, but they greatly increase the likelihood that you'll be focused and ready. In fact, on the day of a performance, your skill and fitness levels are set. The only piece of your performance that you can adjust is your mindset, and routines help you slip into a mindset that will optimize your performance.

Now, think about your own funnel and write a pre-performance or pre-practice routine for yourself. Look at the pre-performance and pre-practice routines that Lois and Asif wrote. In Lois's case, the performance is a big test she's taking that day.

Lois's Pre-Performance Routine	Asif's Pre-Practice Routine
On the drive to school, I'll talk to the other girls in the car pool but not about the test. Once I'm at school, I'll go to my classroom early. I'll sit in the back of the room and listen to my favorite tunes while I read through my study notes. Once the bell rings, I'll go to my seat, take out my earbuds, and sing to myself the tune I was just playing. As I sing to myself, I'll take out my pencil and eraser. I'll do some neck stretches to relax my neck and shoulders. I'll then close my eyes and imagine going through the test as I answer questions. I'll imagine hitting a test question I don't know the answer to but moving on. I'll then imagine coming back to the question as the answer comes to me.	On the drive to practice, I'll think about two practice objectives I want to focus on that day. I'll arrive at least 30 minutes early and go through my personal stretches. As the other guys arrive, I'll hang out with them for a few minutes and then walk the court. As I stretch out with the team, I'll listen to my "get pumped" music. I'll talk to coach when he arrives and stand next to him for a few minutes. He always says something encouraging to me. I'll then run up and down the sidelines until coach calls us out for drills. As I walk onto the court I'll remind myself to focus on my two practice objectives. I'll close my eyes and go through my mistake recovery plan at least six times.

Pre-performance or pre-practice routines aren't cast in stone. Feel free to evaluate and periodically adjust your routines from one practice or performance to the next. If a routine doesn't improve your focus, modify it or replace it until you find a routine that does.

-🔅- *STRESS HACK:* An interesting thing about remembering what you learned is that you're more likely to remember something in the place where you learned it. If you took your history exam in a lecture-style classroom with big windows, you may recall what you learned best in that same or a very similar classroom. Obviously, you can't stage your bedroom with desks and a whiteboard, but you can make a similar environment by regulating temperature, smells, and noises. If you're going to take a test at a desk, study at a desk, not in bed. If the classroom is warm, study at home in a warm room. Wear the same soothing fragrance during the recital that you wore during piano practice. The closer you make the test or performance environment to the practice environment, the better you'll remember what you learned.

🌰 *IN A NUTSHELL*

The stress you feel in games, recitals, and tests is primarily performance stress. You want to do well and you're worried and stressed that you might not. The skills in this chapter work for any performance: dating, a practice or game, a school report, a job interview, a recital, or a play. Learning skills to handle performance stress will not only reduce your stress but will likely improve your performance, too.

CHAPTER 5
Family and Friend Stress

Family and friends can be a great source of support, but they can be a great source of stress, too. There are the arguments with parents and disagreements with siblings. There are the friends who push you around or who blame you for something you didn't do. Learning skills to manage family and friend stress will increase your confidence that you can handle difficult conversations, difficult people, and build solid and lasting relationships over time. These skills work for any relationship: family, friends, teachers, even the crotchety next-door neighbor. In this chapter, you'll learn the following skills to manage family and friend stress:

- Communicate Calmly and Clearly
- Walk Down the Conflict Staircase
- Think It Through to the End
- Begin with a Sincere Apology
- Solve Problems Rather than Stress about Them
- Stand Up for Yourself
- Take Feedback Like a Pro
- Move to Another Seat
- De-Magnify to De-Stress
- Hope for the Best, Plan for the Most Likely

Communicate Calmly and Clearly

Learning to communicate calmly and clearly with people is an important stress management skill. Communicating clearly strengthens relationships so that you're less prone to feel stressed when a relationship hits a bump. Communicating clearly can also help you avoid arguments with people that fuel stress, as well as build new friendships with people you meet.

The 4 Cs of Calm and Clear Communication

Clear communication involves more than what you say. It involves how you sound and look when you say it. To communicate clearly, it's important that your body and voice match the message your words are sending. The 4Cs of clear communication can help make sure that people get the right message.

THE 4 Cs OF CALM AND CLEAR COMMUNICATION

	Don't . . .	Do . . .
Calm voice	Mumble Shout or yell	Speak calmly and at a volume suitable to the environment
Calm body	Clench your fists or point at the person Slouch Turn away from the person	Try a half-smile Stand tall Face the person
Connect with your eyes	Look down or away Squint	Maintain eye contact Open your eyes and raise your eyebrows
Create space	Get in the person's face Lean in too close to the person	Keep an arm's length from the person Lean back a little

Try practicing the 4Cs in front of a mirror in private. First try the *Don'ts*. How did that look and feel? Now try the *Do's*. How did that look and feel?

Sending Clear Messages

Communication is about sending messages, and calm and clear communication is about sending messages that people understand and are open to receiving. Often, people send You-messages, and You-messages can make communicating with someone more difficult, particularly when you use words like *never, should,* or *always*. You-messages can put people on the defensive. When you say to a friend, "You never listen to me," it sounds as if you're attacking them. When you send You-messages, people stop listening and sometimes get upset. And upset people can stress you out!

I-messages, on the other hand, help you clearly and honestly express yourself. I-messages tend to put people at ease because it sounds as if it's about you and not about them (even when sometimes it is about them). Using I-messages rather than You-messages improves your relationships with friends and family, and stronger relationships means less worry that you'll lose friends or upset people. An I-message includes three parts:

- **I feel . . .** This is the most important part of an I-message because you immediately signal to the listener that you're not going to put them on the spot. You draw in the listener rather than push them away. Now the person is listening.

- **When you . . .** Next, you describe the facts. In this part of the I-message, you describe specifically what happened. It works best to describe what you actually observed, rather than your opinion or interpretation.

- **Because . . .** Last, you describe the reason you're feeling what you're feeling. In this part, you describe the effect of the person's actions on you. This is important feedback for the listener, particularly if you don't want the person to do what they did again.

SEND I-MESSAGES TO COMMUNICATE CALMLY AND CLEARLY

Situation	You-message	I-message
You're stressed because Olivia is sitting with Madeleine on the bus and they don't invite you to join them.	"You *never* sit and talk with me on the bus anymore."	"**I feel** hurt **when you** sit with Madeleine on the bus and don't invite me to join **because** it makes me think that you don't want to be my friend anymore."
You're upset because your friend Justin picked Devon for his team and didn't pick you.	"You should pick me because I'm your best friend, not Devon."	"**I felt** upset **when you** picked Devon without asking me **because** it makes me think that I'm not your best friend anymore."
You're stressed because your mom asked you to clean your room and your friends are waiting for you at the mall.	"You *always* ask me to do things when I have plans with my friends."	"**I feel** frustrated **when you** ask me to do something when I have plans with my friends, **because** it makes me think that you don't care whether I have friends or not."

Now, think of several situations and write a You-message and then an I-message for each situation. Practice both messages in front of the mirror in private. How did each message make you feel?

WALK DOWN THE
CONFLICT STAIRCASE

Conflict is stressful . . . and sometimes it's *very* stressful. But it's also impossible to avoid. You say the wrong thing and it upsets a friend, or you don't hear your dad speak to you and before you know it, he tells you that you're grounded. You can't always avoid conflict. But you can learn to defuse it.

Conflict is a bit like a staircase. You can climb up the stairs to escalate conflict, or you can climb down the stairs to defuse it. A kid gives you a weird look and you glare at him. You just took a step up the conflict staircase. Your sister teases you and you tease her back. You just took a step up the conflict staircase. Your mom tells you to stop doing something and you insist you weren't doing it. You just took a step up the conflict staircase.

Active listening can help you climb down the conflict staircase. Active listening is more than hearing what the speaker is saying. Active listening is understanding what the speaker is saying and then communicating back to the speaker that you understand. It includes three basic strategies:

- **Listen carefully to what the person is saying.** Listen verbally and non-verbally. Say "Yes," or "Mmm hmm," and smile. Nod your head to encourage the speaker to continue. Try not to form opinions or judgements, as these interfere with fully understanding what the speaker is trying to communicate to you.

- **Repeat what the person said to the you.** Repeating or paraphrasing communicates to the speaker that you heard what they said. Repeating also creates an opportunity for the speaker to correct or elaborate on what they said.

- **Clarify the point the person is making.** Rather than saying, "I didn't do it," or "You don't understand," try, "What do you mean?" or "Why do you think that?" This gives the other person time to explain their point or the problem and, more importantly, gives you time to understand their point or why it's a problem for them. Once the other person clarifies the point, you'll have a better chance to present the facts.

STRESS HACK: Before you can resolve a conflict, it's necessary first to decide what you want to accomplish. Are you trying to change someone's mind about something? Are you defending yourself or a loved one? What's more important: the issue or the person? If you can't answer these questions, then why are you involving yourself in the conflict? Maybe the best thing to do is drop it. Also, no matter how well you argue your case, there's always a chance that you won't get what you want. If that happens, you may want to cut your losses and walk away. A good way to end a conflict is to agree to disagree. This means that you and the other person are willing to live with the fact that you have different opinions, different goals, and different ways of going about things. Life goes on and there's no point in dwelling on what did or didn't happen, or who is right or wrong.

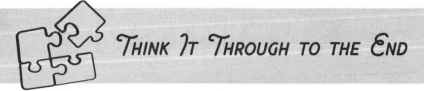

THINK IT THROUGH TO THE END

Acting before thinking through what might happen can be stressful. When you say something to friends before you think through how they might react, you can upset or even lose friends—or worry that you might next time. That's stressful! When you go out with friends before asking your parents if it's okay, you might end up grounded for the weekend. That's stressful. Acting before thinking can make you miss out on friends, fun, and sometimes bigger things in the future, such as college and a good job. But with practice, you can learn to think ahead calmly and clearly before you act on a decision.

Think back to a recent time you acted before you thought it through to the end. Recall who was there, what you were doing, and what the other people were doing. Then, follow these steps to learn to think it through to the end:

1. Identify what you wanted at that moment.

2. Identify what the other person or people wanted at that moment.

3. Describe what happened. What did you do? What did the other person do?

4. Describe the stressful troubles or consequences that happened to you.

5. Think through what you could have done differently in the situation.

To see how to do this, check out Lois's *Think It Through to the End Exercise.*

LOIS'S THINK IT THROUGH TO THE END EXERCISE

What did you want at that moment?

I wanted Jessica to spend Saturday afternoon with me.

What did the other person or people want at that moment?

Jessica wanted to spend time with her cousins before they flew back home.

What happened? What did you do? What did the other person or people do?

I texted Jessica nonstop. She told me that she wouldn't see her cousins for a year and that we could hang out together on Sunday. I just kept texting her.

What happened after you acted before you thought it through to the end?

Jessica stopped returning my texts which freaked me out. I nearly had a panic attack. I finally stopped texting her but I was so stressed out I couldn't sleep that night.

What could you have done differently to avoid these stressful consequences?

I could have given Jessica some space. She's really nice and is helping me get to know other kids at school. She even offered to see me Sunday. I could have said yes, and perhaps asked her to text me a couple of times on Saturday to tell me what she was doing. I think she would have liked that. I know she would have done that if I had asked her nicely.

BEGIN WITH A SINCERE APOLOGY

Conflicts, disagreements, and misunderstandings are stressful, and nothing fixes this kind of stress faster than a sincere apology. A sincere apology calms the other person and signals that you're ready to fix the problem and to learn from it. The first step in learning to make a sincere apology is to understand what *isn't* a sincere apology:

- **Empty apology.** "I'm sorry. I said I was sorry. What more do you want from me?" The empty apology feels insincere because it has no substance. It's the apology you offer when you think the other person is wrong. This kind of apology is an empty attempt to move on rather than a true attempt to understand and to repair.

- **Deflected apology.** "I'm sorry this happened," or "I'm sorry you feel that way." The deflected apology fails to take responsibility for hurting or upsetting someone. You blame the situation or the person rather than owning your share (at least) of the problem. This kind of apology leaves the other person wondering whether you apologized at all.

- **Denial apology.** "I'm sorry, but it wasn't my fault," or "I didn't mean to hurt you, but I'm sorry if I did." The denial apology is all smoke and mirrors. If you pretend you didn't do something wrong, then it isn't necessary for you to apologize, right? This kind of apology leaves the other person more upset than before you apologized.

- **Excessive apology.** "Oh my gosh, I'm so sorry. I can't believe I did that. I am so, so, so, so sorry. What can I do to make it up to you? Will you ever forgive me? I'm so sorry. I'm the worst." The excessive apology, at first glance, seems well-intentioned. But the excessive apology diverts attention from what you did. This kind of apology leaves the other person without a way to feel better because it's now about your feelings and not about theirs.

Now that you know what isn't a sincere apology, follow these steps to make a sincere apology:

HOW TO APOLOGIZE

Step 1:	Say what you're sorry for.	I'm sorry for ...
Step 2:	Say why it was wrong.	It was wrong because ...
Step 3:	Accept full responsibility.	I accept full responsibility for what I did (said).
Step 4:	Ask how you can make it better.	How can I make this better?
Step 5:	Commit to not do it again.	I promise that I won't do it again.
Step 6:	Ask for forgiveness.	Will you forgive me?

Look at the following examples of sincere apologies. Do they include all six steps?

Situation	Sincere Apology
Alesandro's dad told him that he could play soccer with friends after he finished his homework. Instead, Alesandro finished some but not all his homework and went to the soccer field.	I'm sorry, Dad. You told me that I couldn't play soccer with my friends until I completed all my homework, but I went before I was done anyway. It was wrong because you trusted me to do what you asked and I didn't do it. I accept full responsibility for what I did. How can I make this up to you? I promise that I won't do it again. Will you forgive me?
Kanesha's mom told her to change her shirt before she left the house. Instead, Kanesha left wearing the shirt her mom asked her to change.	I'm sorry, Mom. You told me to change my shirt but I didn't do it. It was wrong of me to ignore you; I should've talked to you about it instead. That's my fault. How can I make this better? I promise I won't ignore what you tell me again. Will you forgive me?

Situation	Sincere Apology
Asif's teacher asked him to stay after class so that he could speak to him about his math grade. Instead, Asif left class with friends while his teacher waited for him.	I'm sorry, Mr. Sarafian. You asked me to stay after class to talk to you about my math grade. I know it was wrong to leave you hanging like that because you're busy and you wanted to meet with me to see if you could help me with my math grade. I accept full responsibility for what I did. Is there a way that I can make this up to you? I promise that I'll meet with you if you're willing to meet with me again. Will you forgive me and give me a second chance?
Kanesha's older sister, Alicia, asked her not to borrow her clothes. Instead, Kanesha borrowed one of her sister's sweaters for photo day at school.	I'm sorry, Alicia. You told me not to borrow your clothes without asking you first but I did it anyway. That was wrong of me and I accept full responsibility for what I did. Is there a way to make up for this? I promise not to borrow your things again without asking you first. Will you forgive me?

-⚙- *STRESS HACK:* Friendships can be stressful, even when they're going well. It doesn't take much to protect and strengthen friendships, but it does take some of your time and caring. Not only that, giving to your friendships feels good and encourages your friends to give to you. There are many small ways that you can give to your friends. You can compliment a friend's clothing or basketball shot. You can give your full attention, in the moment, to what a friend is saying. You can share your lunch or attend the game of someone you know but not well. Best of all, you can give calmness to a friend who is stressed or frustrated.

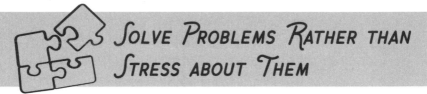

Solve Problems Rather than Stress about Them

If you're like most people, you run into a problem now and then, and when you do, it can be stressful. Maybe your mom asked you to clean your room, but you don't know how you'll squeeze that in with all the other things you're supposed to do. Maybe your friends are pressuring you to use alcohol or drugs. Maybe your sister keeps borrowing your clothes without asking your permission first. Problems are stressful, but they're even more stressful when you don't have a good way to solve them. The **ICCAN** skill is a great way to solve problems and is just four steps:

1. *I***dentify the problem.** A good way to do this is to ask yourself, "What's the problem? What is it that I'm trying to solve?" If you're not sure what the problem is, try asking others how they would define the problem. Lois decided to use **ICCAN** to solve the problem of not having any friends in her new school.

2. *C***hoices that might help.** After you identify the problem, brainstorm a list of possible choices or solutions. It's best to come up with as many choices as possible, no matter how silly they may be. Brainstorming is all about quantity not quality, so don't throw away any choices when you brainstorm. You'll decide in the next step which choice is likely to be a good or bad one. With some practice, you can find a solution that solves, manages, or at least improves most problems. Lois brainstormed a great list of possible choices or solutions to the problem of no friends in her new school. The "wear a sign" choice was silly but that's what brainstorming is about.

3. *C***osts and benefits of each choice.** After you list all the possible choices, the next step is to list the costs and benefits for each choice or solution. When it comes to possible choices that involve people,

it helps to think through the possible costs to other people of each choice. To consider possible costs to other people, ask yourself the following questions:

- How would the person feel if I did this?
- What might the person do if I did this?
- What else might happen?

4. *A*pply a choice. Next, select one of the choices and try it. The best choice is the one that's most likely to work and least likely to create problems for you. There's seldom a perfect solution to a problem, but there are many good solutions that can help a little and not make things worse. Also, you can't know whether a choice works until you try it. Lois decided to introduce herself to the girl in her English class. This is a great choice because it's likely to work and isn't likely to create bigger problems for Lois. Lois even developed a plan to do this; she'll compliment the girl on her taste in earrings.

5. *N*ow review how well the choice worked. The final step is to review how well the choice or solution worked. To help you evaluate how well a solution worked, think about it like a target. A bullseye is when the choice works great. This means that you got what you wanted AND it didn't cause you any problems.

If the choice was a bullseye, this means that you'll remember to use this choice again in similar situations. If the choice hit the target but wasn't a bullseye, this means that you'll want to modify the choice a little. For example, if the girl wasn't in class that day, then Lois will find the girl at lunch and introduce herself there. Also, sometimes adding a skill you've learned can change a good choice into a bullseye choice. For example, communicating calmly and clearly, standing up for yourself, or beginning with a sincere apology can change a good choice into a bullseye. At other times, just adding a kind word or a compliment can improve the choice. Lois decided to compliment the girl's taste in earrings. Compliments are great ice breakers too!

If the choice missed the target completely, this means that the choice didn't work at all or, worse yet, created more problems for you. Throw that choice out the window and either select another choice from the list or brainstorm other choices. Sometimes trying one choice leads you to other choices that you didn't think of the first time.

LOIS'S ICCAN EXERCISE

Step 1: Identify the problem.

No friends in new school.

Step 2: Choices that might help.

Choice 1: Introduce myself to the girl sitting next to me in English class.

Choice 2: Wait for girls to introduce themselves to me during or after classes.

Choice 3: Ask the school counselor to introduce me to some girls at school.

Choice 4: Walk around with a sign on my back that says, "Hi, I'm Lois!"

Step 3: Costs and benefits of each choice.

Choice 1: Introduce myself to the girl sitting next to me in English class.

Costs: It feels kind of weird, and what if the girl ignores me? Ouch!

Benefits: The girl is nice and she's popular, so she might introduce me to more kids.

Choice 2: Wait for girls to introduce themselves to me during or after classes.

Costs: Might take forever to make friends, and they might think I'm stuck-up.

Benefits: I don't have to feel weird or take a chance of them rejecting me.

Choice 3: Ask the school counselor to introduce me to some girls at school.

Costs: Sends the wrong message to the other kids. Really, the counselor?

Benefits: I don't have to introduce myself, which feels kind of weird.

Choice 4: Walk around with a sign on my back that says, "Hi, I'm Lois!"

Costs: Definitely a choice that will make life harder. I'll feel super weird.

Benefits: A sign will definitely get their attention. It's creative and that's me!

Step 4: Apply a choice.

I'll introduce myself to the girl in English class. I'll compliment her earrings.

Step 5: Now review how well the choice worked.

Bullseye! I have a new friend! We talked about earrings and she said she liked the earrings I was wearing too. She's really nice and invited me to sit with her and her friends at lunch.

> " Making new friends in high school is tough, and my new high school is huge. I didn't know how I was going to make new friends in a school so big. I decided to try ICCAN. Just sitting down and brainstorming the possible ways I could solve the problem of no friends in the school helped me feel less overwhelmed. ICCAN made making new friends a lot easier.
> —Lois "

Stand Up for Yourself

When you're stressed, it can be difficult to stand up for yourself, but not standing up for yourself can make your life even more stressful. Your friends ask you to hang out after school, but you really need to work on a big essay that's due tomorrow. But you're worried that they won't invite you to hangout again if you say no, so you say yes. Now you're worried that you won't have enough time to finish the essay. Or, your mom asks you to watch your younger sister while she shops, but you don't know how you'll watch your sister and finish all your homework too. Learning to stand up for yourself and say no thank you can help you feel less powerless, less stressed, and better about yourself.

It takes a lot of skill to stand up for yourself, particularly when you're stressed. **DEAL** can help. **DEAL** stands for **D**escribe, **E**xpress, **A**sk, and **L**ist. **DEAL** can help you stand up for yourself, ask for help, and manage conflicts. It's important to follow these steps in a calm and respectful way:

*D*escribe the problem. When you're talking to someone, tell them what the problem is. For example, "This is the third time you told me you would help me with my homework but you keep bailing out at the last minute."

*E*xpress how the problem makes you feel, without blaming the other person. For example, "Once or twice is okay, but three times hurts my feelings because I start to think you don't care."

*A*sk for a change that you hope will fix the problem. For example, "How about we agree that you don't say you're gonna help me with my homework if you can't really do that."

*L*ist how you think the change is going to improve your situation, or fix the problem. This will motivate the person to try out your idea. For example, "If you tell me straight up that you can't help me, then I'll know that I need to get help from someone else."

One last point about using **DEAL** to stand up for yourself. After you go through the four steps of **DEAL**, get the buy-in. For example, ask the other person, "Would that work for you?" or "Would you do that for me?" The buy-in is important. It makes the other person have to say no to you. This final step puts you in a position of power rather than powerlessness.

> **"** My plate is totally full this week. I have a big history exam to study for, and I need to spend more time working on my essay for AP English. Also, it's my sister's birthday, and my mom asked me to help her prep for the party. I was already feeling overwhelmed by the number of things on my plate and then Mr. Wong asked whether I would be willing to tutor a couple of his students in chemistry this week. I didn't want to say no to Mr. Wong. He's helped me a lot with my college applications! But I knew that saying no was the right thing to do and I used DEAL to do it. Mr. Wong was totally cool with it and even thanked me for telling him that my plate was too full to take on a tutoring gig.
> —Kanesha **"**

☀️ *STRESS HACK:* Sometimes it helps to package your assertive statement so it's a little more appetizing to the person. This is the stand-up sandwich. It's not always possible to use a stand-up sandwich, but it works great when you can. A stand-up sandwich includes a nice comment (the slice of bread) on either side of the assertive request (the stuff between the slices). Beginning with something nice gets the person's attention. Ending with something nice makes it more difficult for them to say no to the assertive request. Here's how it works. *Bread*: "I love your taste in clothes!" *Stuff Inside*: "But stop kidding me about my sweater." *Bread*: "You always look great. Let's go shopping this Saturday. You can help me find clothes that we both like." The trick to the stand-up sandwich is to be honest and sincere. If you can't think of something nice to say that is true about the person, it's better just to ask for what you want calmly and politely.

☀️ *STRESS HACK:* Sometimes people don't respond the way you want the first time you DEAL. Perhaps they didn't hear you or perhaps they're not accustomed to you standing up for yourself. Either way, don't give up too soon. Hit the repeat button! Keep repeating the assertive request. You can change it around a little, but keep repeating the request in a calm, clear, polite, and direct way until the person agrees or walks away. For example, "I'd like to help but I can't do it today," or, "How about tomorrow? I could help you then," or, "I'll help tomorrow. Let's put it on our calendars."

TAKE FEEDBACK LIKE A PRO

Taking feedback can be stressful. Whether it's from a friend who shares his opinion about your new shoes, or whether it's from your mom who tells you how to do the laundry in a particular way, feedback is a natural part of learning. One of the things that can make feedback stressful is if you tend to hear and focus on only the "negative" part of the feedback rather than taking in the bigger picture, which often includes the many things you did well. If you tend to lock on the negative when someone is giving you feedback, try taking feedback like a pro:

- **Stay calm.** The moment you notice that someone is giving or about to give you feedback, stop and take a calming breath. It only takes a second to center yourself and relax. Calm your face, too, in order to counter an automatic smirk or quick dismissive eye roll.

- **Remind yourself of the benefits of feedback.** Feedback, when it's constructive, helps you improve your skills, better your relationships, and become more successful in all the areas of your life. In most cases, people give you feedback because they want to help you be the best person you can be. Taking feedback can be tough, especially when the person giving you feedback could use a little feedback themselves. However, even imperfect people can give you helpful feedback.

- **Listen and don't interrupt.** Listen closely to what they have to say. Often, when people receive feedback, they're not really listening. They're thinking of comebacks or arguments to what the person is saying, which means they're not hearing what the person really means. If you notice that you're thinking about what you're going to say next, pause and then repeat back what you heard the person say, "I hear you saying that you like me better in lavender than in green, is that right?" Remember to smile and nod to signal that you're listening and open to hearing more. Also, it helps to remember that *giving* feedback isn't always easy, either. Your friend may feel nervous sharing her opinion with you. She may trip over her words or not communicate her thoughts clearly. Smiling and nodding will put the person at ease, which will make it easier for the person to give you helpful feedback so that you learn from it.

Also, repeat back to the person the compliments and good things you hear: "You like that I'm always on time," or, "You're pleased with the way I straightened my closet." This can help you remain calm, open, and positive.

- **Thank the person.** After the person gives you feedback, look them in the eyes and thank them for it: "I really appreciate that you took the time to share this with me." When you thank the person for feedback, you signal to them that you've heard what they said and that you're open to learning from it. Thanking the person for feedback is the opposite of being defensive, and the person will get that. Thanking them for the feedback doesn't mean that they're right and you're wrong. Nor does it mean that you agree with the feedback and you must act on it. It just means you heard what the person said. Remember, they cared enough about this and about you to mention it to you.

- **Ask questions to understand.** The best feedback is clear enough that you can follow through with the suggestions people make. You're not arguing or debating but asking questions that help you understand the problem and how you can go about fixing it. Ask for specific examples, "You don't like to ask repeatedly for me to do something. When was the last time this happened?" or "You said that I interrupted you. What were we talking about when I interrupted you?" Also, it helps to ask whether this was a single situation or a pattern. For example, you might ask, "Have you noticed me interrupting other people?" Last, ask for suggestions to correct the problem or address the feedback in some way: "You said that lavender isn't my best color. What colors do you think look good on me?"

-⚙- *STRESS HACK:* Fogging is a simple skill that helps you accept feedback calmly without feeling upset or stressed. To fog feedback, imagine a cloud of thick, dense fog between you and the other person. As the person gives you feedback, imagine the words slowing down in the fog as they come at you. You can even imagine the words absorbing the fog so that they grow into fluffy, non-threatening puffballs of feedback.

---

66 I tried fogging with my dad last night when I asked him for help with my essay. He's not the best communicator in the world. He started to go on and on about the topic and how I hadn't organized the material clearly. I knew he was trying to help but I started to get annoyed. So I imagined that I was sitting in a cloud of fog. Every time he said something, I imagined his words coming at me, entering the fog, and slowing down. I even imagined his words absorbing some of the fog and puffing up and then disappearing. Fogging his feedback made it a lot easier for me to take in his actual suggestions, which, fine, weren't that bad.

—Alesandro

99

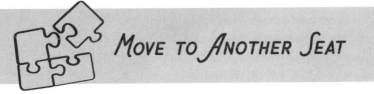

MOVE TO ANOTHER SEAT

Imagine you're seated in a large theater. You look around and notice that depending on where you sit, you have different views or perspectives of the stage. There's the mezzanine, the orchestra, the balcony. Every perspective is a bit different and, for that reason, you have a different experience of the performance. This works for your mind too. Your emotional mind can repeatedly jump to particular assumptions or explanations that cause you to feel unnecessarily stressed and anxious. This is particularly true when the event is ambiguous and you could interpret it in several ways. For example, you might interpret a look on someone's face to mean that they think you're weird, then you feel anxious and stressed. Maybe they think this or maybe they don't. How do you know for sure? But once your emotional mind latches onto a particular view of an event, it can be tough to let go of it.

But this doesn't mean you can't learn to loosen your emotional mind's grip on a particular view of the situation. In fact, you can probably view any situation from another perspective if you try, and learning to change how you see things can help you feel less stressed. To feel less stressed and anxious about an event or situation, follow these steps to move to another seat:

1. On a blank sheet of paper, briefly describe the stressful event along with your view of the event.

2. Rate the degree (0–100%, where 100% means you completely believe) that you believe your view of the event is correct.

3. Brainstorm five to ten other possible views or explanations for the event.

4. Rate the likelihood that each alternative explanation is true (0–100%, where 100% means it's completely true or accurate).

5. Re-rate the degree (0–100%) that you believe the negative interpretation is correct.

To see how to do this, check out the Ofelia's *Move to Another Seat Exercise.* She was feeling stressed when her best friend wasn't returning her texts.

OFELIA'S MOVE TO ANOTHER SEAT EXERCISE

Describe the stressful event or situation:	I've been texting Melody for an hour and she's not returning any of my texts.
Describe your view of the stressful event or situation:	Melody isn't returning my texts because she never wants to speak to me again.

How strongly do I believe my initial view of the event is true (0 to 100)?:   95

How stressed does this view make me feel (0 to 100)?:   80

Alternative views of the stressful event or situation:	*How likely is view true (0–100%)*
Melody isn't returning my texts because she's studying for her math final. She's freaking out about that and that's all she can think about right now.	75%
Melody isn't returning my texts because she's in a dead zone and her phone isn't receiving my texts now.	25%
Melody isn't returning my texts because she wants me to calm down a little. Last time we talked, she said that I was too upset to think straight and I needed to calm down a little before we talked again.	95%
Melody isn't returning my texts because she lost or broke her phone.	15%
Melody isn't returning my texts because her parents grounded her and took away her phone.	5%

How strongly do I believe my initial view of the event is true now (0 to 100)?:   30

How stressed does this view make me feel now (0 to 100)?:   20

" I use the Move to Another Seat skill a lot. I realized that I almost always assume that my friends are mad at me for some little thing or another. Sure, I'm not perfect and sometimes my friends want a little break from me. Hey, I want a little break from them sometimes too. But my friends are great and they're always there for me. They're never upset with me for no reason and even if they were, I know we could talk about it. Learning to move to another seat in my emotional mind has helped me feel less stressed about my friendships and about other people in my life too.

—Ofelia **"**

DE-MAGNIFY TO DE-STRESS

When you're feeling stressed or anxious, it could be because you've magnified an event and lost sight of the bigger picture. Magnifying an event is like looking at the event through the magnifying end of binoculars. It makes the event look bigger than it really is. An argument with a friend looks like the end of a friendship. A C on a math test looks like you'll flunk out of school. Your parents grounding you for the weekend looks like the end of your social life.

To de-magnify an event, try looking at the event through the other end of the binoculars. This means you step back and see the bigger picture. Follow these steps to de-magnify to de-stress:

1. On a blank sheet of paper, briefly describe the stressful event.

2. Next, describe the magnified view of the event. Zoom in and think about the event as if it's the most important thing in the world, and all the potential consequences. Rate the level of stress you feel (where *H* is high, *M* is medium, and *L* is low) when you view the event through the magnified end of the binoculars. Write **H**, **M**, or **L** next to the magnified view.

3. Next, describe a de-magnified view of the event. Step back and think about the situation in the context of your life, and what else might be coming into play. What are more realistic outcomes? Rate the level of stress you feel (where *H* is high, *M* is medium, and *L* is low) when you view the event through the de-magnified end of the binoculars and consider the bigger picture. Write **H**, **M**, or **L** next to the de-magnified view.

Check out Kanesha's *De-Magnify to De-Stress Exercise* to see how she de-magnified several events to feel less stressed.

KANESHA'S DE-MAGNIFY TO DE-STRESS EXERCISE

Event: Forgot my sister's birthday.

Magnified View		**De-Magnified View**	
She'll hate me and never want to do anything fun with me.	H	She'll probably feel a little hurt but she'll get over it if I apologize.	M

Event: Argument with best friend.

Magnified View		**De-Magnified View**	
I've lost the best friend I'll ever have in my life.	H	We've had arguments before but we always make up.	M

Event: Missed a pass during the big field hockey game.

Magnified View		**De-Magnified View**	
Coach will bench me for life and I'll never play on the team again.	H	Coach doesn't bench a player for life because of one missed pass.	L

Event: Dropped lunch tray in the cafeteria.

Magnified View		**De-Magnified View**	
I'm so embarrassed. People will never forget it!	M	Everyone does embarrassing things and people get over it.	L

Event: Burned the cake for the family party.

Magnified View		**De-Magnified View**	
I ruined the family party.	M	There were plenty of other desserts and people liked the dip I made.	L

Event: Parents grounded me Saturday night.

Magnified View		**De-Magnified View**	
My parents grounded me for the weekend. I'll lose all my friends.	H	All my friends miss a weekend now and then and we're okay.	L

⇐ *TRY IT HERE TOO:* You can de-magnify to de-stress for almost any event that stresses you out, not just for family and friend stress. You can de-magnify getting a bad grade on a test or having an argument with your significant other. You can de-magnify missing a pass during a soccer game or a hitting a wrong note during the holiday concert. You can even de-magnify a poor night of sleep or when someone trashes one of your social media posts. No matter how big an event may feel in the moment, there's likely a way to de-magnify it and see the bigger picture.

STRESS HACK: When you're stressed, you tend to get stuck in one stressful thought after another. A fun way to get unstuck from a stressful thought is to take the long way around it by describing the stressful thought with a longer, wordier description. For example, to take the long way around the stressful thought: *"What if I fail the quiz tomorrow?"* say to yourself, *"My mind is once again having that very familiar and oh so stressful thought—a thought that enters my mind over and over again, in the same way, in spite of me knowing that it's not true—that I'll fail the quiz tomorrow."* Taking the long way around a stressful thought creates some distance between you and the thought so that you can see things as they really are rather than how you think they are.

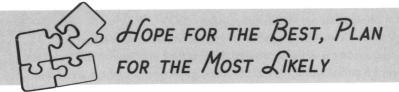

Hope for the Best, Plan for the Most Likely

Have you heard the saying, "Hope for the best, plan for the worst"? Well, it's a great attitude when the worst is likely to happen. However, planning for the worst when the worst isn't likely to happen is a waste of time. Why plan for something that likely won't happen, even if it's the worst you can imagine? To feel less stressed, identify what's the most likely thing that could happen and plan for that. After all, if it's the most likely thing that could happen, you want to prepare for it. To hope for the best and plan for the most likely, follow these steps:

1. First, ask yourself *what's the **best** that could happen and how likely is this to happen*. It always helps to consider that there is a best outcome. However, the best thing that could happen may not be any more likely than the worst thing that could happen. For example, if you're stressing about your first date with someone, the best that could happen is that you discover your soulmate who is perfect in every way. Although this would be an awesome outcome for a first date, it's not very likely. Finding a soulmate usually takes more than one first date.

2. Next, ask yourself *what's the **worst** that could happen and how likely is this to happen*. There's a worst outcome too and it's as unlikely as the best outcome. It helps to consider the worst because, as stressed as you might feel about what could happen, it can always be worse. For example, the worst that could happen on your first date might be that the person falls asleep during dinner at the restaurant with you. Although the person might be very tired, it's unlikely that the person will fall asleep in a busy restaurant.

3. Then, ask yourself *what's the most likely that could happen*. To feel less stressed, identify the most likely thing and prepare for it. For example, what's most likely to happen on a first date is that you'll like the person enough to try a second date . . . or dislike the person enough to decide that the first date is the last date.

4. Next, rate how confident (0 to 100%, where 100% means that you're completely confident) you are that you could handle the most likely outcome.

5. Now it's time to develop your plan. The best plans for handling a difficult most likely outcome (like not liking a person enough to want a second date) include four parts:

    -   **Strengths** you have that you've used to handle most of the difficult events in your life. For example, your intelligence, your sense of humor, your ability to think on your feet or to get along with people.
    -   **Actions** you'll take to cope with the event. For example, speak to friends about the situation and get their ideas, or (when necessary) stand up for yourself, or apologize. Many of these actions might be skills in this book.
    -   **Self-talk** you'll use to encourage and reassure yourself that you can handle a difficult most likely event if it happens. For example, you might say to yourself, "I've handled difficult situations like this before, I can handle this now," or, something as simple as, "I can do this!"
    -   **Support** you'll seek. People handle difficult things with the support of caring friends, family members, teachers, or coaches. Some people are great listeners, and others are great problem solvers, and still others might know someone or something that can help.

6. Last, re-rate how confident you are that you could handle the most likely outcome.

Asif decided to apply the Hope for the Best and Plan for the Most Likely skill to meeting his dad on Saturday. Asif had not seen him since his mom and dad divorced a year ago and his dad moved away. Look at Asif's *Hope for the Best, Plan for the Most Likely Exercise* to see how it helped him stress less about the meeting.

ASIF'S HOPE FOR THE BEST PLAN
FOR THE MOST LIKELY EXERCISE

Event I'm Planning for

I'm meeting my dad for lunch and I'm really stressed. I haven't seen him in a year and I don't know what I'm going to say or what it will be like.

What's the very best that could happen? How likely is that?

We'll both feel great and he'll tell me that he's worked everything out with my mom and they're getting back together. Although they get along okay now, my mom has told me many times that there's no way they're getting back together, so it's not likely.

What's the very worst that could happen? How likely is that?

He doesn't show up, and we never talk or see each other again. This isn't likely. Even after my mom and dad split, my dad still called and texted me sometimes.

What's the most likely that could happen?

We both feel a little uncomfortable but we talk things through. He'll apologize for not seeing me more and I'll say it's okay. I'll ask him if we could see each other more often. He'll probably tell me that he'd like to but can't because he lives so far away now.

How confident am I that I can handle this (0–100%)?

55%

Strengths that will help me cope with the most likely?

I'll feel disappointed, but I'm strong and can handle that. I've handled it before. I'm smart, and will think of other ways to stay connected to him. Maybe I can try to visit him sometime too.

What can I do to cope with the most likely?

I'll be assertive and ask to see him more often. I'll stay in touch by sending texts and pictures of what I'm doing, and I'll ask him to text me too. I'll ask someone at the restaurant to take a picture of us together so that I can look at that when I miss him.

What can I say to myself to cope with the most likely?

I'll tell myself that my dad loves me because he contacted me and would see me more often if he lived closer. I'll remind myself that he still calls and texts me.

Who can support me to help me cope with the most likely?

I'll spend more time with Ben and Jake. They don't see their dads as much as they would like so they'll understand how I feel. I'll talk to my older sister. She misses Dad too, and maybe we can plan a trip together to see him. I'll also talk to Coach. He and my dad went to high school together so Coach knows him and always has good ideas about how I can stay in touch with him.

Now, how confident am I that I can handle this (0–100%)?

90%

-⚙- *STRESS HACK:* In a thunderstorm, you might take shelter from the pelting rain, blowing winds, and deadly lightning strikes. Taking shelter when you're stressed, challenged, or upset can help you feel calm and confident that you can safely ride out emotional storms too. A shelter from stress can be anything that provides a feeling of safety and comfort: talking with a special friend, massaging your hands with lotion, wrapping yourself in a soft, warm blanket.

To create a shelter from stress, write at least six things that are soothing, relaxing, or supportive. Now, every day, close your eyes for a few minutes, take a few calming breaths, and softly say to yourself, *I take shelter in* (for example, my special friendships, or the feel of lotion on my hands, or the warmth of my soft blanket). Try this any time you have a free moment: on the bus to school, just before you fall asleep, when cuddling with your pet.

🌰 In a Nutshell

Family and friend stress hits most teens really hard: disagreements, arguments, getting pushed around, and stressing about all the things that might go wrong. Learning skills to manage family and friend stress will build your social confidence and strengthen your relationships. Strong relationships and a confident attitude will make your life less stressful and more rewarding. Also, many of the skills to deal with family and friend stress work well in other areas of your life, such as school, work, athletics, or dating.

CHAPTER 6
Dating and Relationship Stress

Dating and intimate relationships can be both exciting and stressful. There are the first dates that make your heart beat with excitement and anxiety. There are the difficult break-ups, and the hurt that accompanies a broken heart. Then, there are the ups and downs, twists and turns that are part of any relationship. Learning skills to set healthy boundaries, get what you want in relationships, and recover from arguments or break-ups will increase your confidence in new and long-term intimate relationships. In this chapter, you'll learn the following skills to cope with dating and relationship stress:

- Write It Out
- Create a Broken Heart Recovery Plan
- Negotiate to Connect
- Forgive to Move On
- Try Tincture of Time
- Take a Slice of the Responsibility Pizza
- Escape the Tyranny of Should
- Examine Your Circles of Influence
- Accept It Is What It Is
- Build a Support Network

Write It Out

An important way that human beings manage stress and other feelings is through language. Whether that's talking it through with someone who cares, or writing it out in a journal, language helps us make sense of our feelings, identify patterns in the way we think and feel, and gain perspective on a situation and our reactions to it. In other words, writing it out helps us gain distance from what we're feeling because we can't understand something if we're in the middle of it.

All you need to write out your stress and other feelings is a piece of paper and a pen or pencil. However, you may want to write in a journal or a special notebook. That way you keep all your musings and insights in one place where you can periodically re-read them. You can also write in a document on your computer or mobile device—this can be nice even if you also keep a notebook, since sometimes your phone is more accessible in the moment. If writing isn't your thing, you can keep an audio or video journal.

It's best to set aside a specific time, such as after you finish your homework, or on the bus ride to school. But you can also write it out any time you get the urge to, like:

- When you're feeling stressed, worried, sad, or frustrated about something.
- When you don't know what you think or how you feel about something.
- When you can't get something off your mind.
- When you want to share with others what's going on with you.

Get Started

When you set down to write it out, start with a good experience to warm up. It's easier to connect with what you're thinking when you're feeling calm and positive. Try to journal for about 15 minutes each day for 10 days, to experience the full benefits of writing it out, as well as to start to build a habit. Over time, you can cut back to twice a week for a month. You can write about the same experience for several days or about different experiences each day. Try not to over-focus on describing the details of a situation. Writing about what you're thinking and feeling is what really pays off. As you write, you may discover ways that this experience connects with past situations, feelings, and relationships.

OFELIA'S WRITE IT OUT EXERCISE

April 7th,

I'm driving myself crazy. I can't stop stressing about Tim. I know it's all in my head, but I don't think I could handle another break up. I've got to calm down and remember that Tim isn't my ex. So it doesn't make any sense that Tim would treat me the way my ex did. In fact, he's always nice to me and reassures me that he loves me. I'll try to remember the nice things he says rather than worrying about him breaking up with me. That will help.

April 8th,

I talked to Julia today about me and Tim. She reminded me that Tim is totally into me and that I'm worrying about nothing. It helped to hear that. She's right. Tim and I are good right now. She told me that I'd feel less stressed if I focused on what's going on with Tim and me now rather than thinking about what could go wrong in the future. That helped too. I think I'll start to journal a few things that went well between me and Tim every day. That will help me feel less stressed about the relationship but also a lot happier too.

If there's something you're struggling with, or an event that's upsetting or stressful, you can also try writing about it in the *third* person. For example, rather than writing, "Brian said something that hurt *my* feelings today," try writing, "Brian said something that hurt *her* feelings today." Writing in third person provides a new and somewhat removed perspective that can help to raise your head above the storm and to see things as they really are, rather than how they feel in the moment. Write down what you learned about yourself that you want to take forward in your life. If words are hard to find, draw or make a collage to represent what you're thinking and feeling, or combine drawing and writing to capture a fuller experience of the event and how you feel about it. Sometimes it helps to get out of your head a little. For example, "If this feeling was a color (or the weather, a landscape, a piece of music), how would I describe it?"

Re-Read to Remember

Periodically, re-read your journal entries. Re-reading can help you reflect on where you were and how far you've come. Events that felt very stressful at the time can feel less stressful and important with time. Also, re-reading can help you see patterns in how you think and feel. Recognizing these patterns helps you watch for and sidestep the unhelpful ones.

STRESS HACK: One of the things people love about music is the way it can trigger memories that make us feel sad, or happy, or excited, or invincible. You can use music to help you journal. If a song triggers a strong feeling from your past (for example, stress, hurt, disappointment, sadness, guilt), replay the song a few times and write what comes up for you. Often, just putting your thoughts and feelings down on paper provides some perspective that can help you feel better.

CREATE A BROKEN HEART RECOVERY PLAN

No one likes to have their hearts broken. But if you want to find the right person, you have to take a chance that this person or that person might break your heart. For some teens, the hurt of that first broken heart causes them to worry and stress so much that they avoid trying again. That's where a broken heart recovery plan comes in. When you have a plan to recover more quickly from a broken heart, you'll be more willing to get back into the dating scene. Not only that, as you become more confident that you can recover from breakups, you're more willing to take care of yourself in the relationship you're in. A broken heart recovery plan includes two parts:

Soothe

The soothe part of your broken heart recovery plan includes many of the coping skills in this book. Here are a few of the skills that can help the most:

Breathe slowly and deeply	Replace hopelessness with hope
De-magnify to de-stress	Slip into the present moment
Forgive to move on	Spend time with your best self
Accept it is what it is	Touch hand to heart
Move mindfully	Try tincture of time
Move to another seat	Write it out
Relax your body	Take a slice of the responsibility pie

The soothe part of your plan also includes other healthy ways you've taken care of yourself in the past when you've been hurt. Spending time in nature might have been the way you've taken care of yourself in the past, or arts and crafts projects, or spending more time with your pets. Soothing activities can be anything, as long as they're healthy, safe, and have helped soothe you in the past. Don't forget to soothe your senses, too. Fragrant candles, favorite songs, and a favorite sweater are all great ways to soothe a body in which beats a hurting heart.

Support

The support part of your broken heart recovery plan is important too. Seeking support is a great way to get through any tough time, particularly the time it takes to heal a broken heart. Support is anyone who will listen and be there for you. Write the names and how to reach them in your broken heart recovery plan so that the information is at your fingertips. You don't want to hunt down a phone number when your heart is broken. Also, think back to how the people helped in the past so that you can ask them to help in that way again. Here are several ideas for support:

- **Friends who supported you during difficult times in the past.** Perhaps the best sources of support are the friends you've leaned on in the past. These are the great listeners in your life. Since they've helped you through difficult times in the past, they know what works for you and what doesn't. You also know what to tell them and what not to tell them because you've been to this rodeo together before.

- **New friends.** Friends can come and go. Your best friend might move out of state, or several of your close friends might go to a different high school. This happens, so it's important to build your friendship network with new people who can be there for you, just in case. Remember, support is what feels supportive to you, so don't be shy about telling people what you want and what works for you.

- **Family members.** Family can be a great source of support, but perhaps not every member of your family. If your mom or dad is a great listener, add their names to your plan. Or maybe your older sibling has dealt with their own broken heart and is willing to listen and to share with you what they've learned about healing. Perhaps you have a favorite grandparent or aunt or uncle. But remember that just because they're your family doesn't mean that they're the best listeners. You'll want to lean on family members that help you heal.

- **Teachers, members of your religious community, school counselors.** There are likely other people in your life who are comforting sources of support. Perhaps you could share how you're feeling with a favorite teacher or the school counselor. Perhaps you could talk to a member of your church choir or the leader of your religious community for a bit of reassurance, comfort, or a kind word.

Now it's time to put together your broken heart recovery plan. Check out what *Alesandro's Broken Heart Recovery Plan* looks like. It's great to have a plan, and it's even better to review it from time to time, particularly if you're in the dating scene. Feel free to update your plan with new skills or ideas any time you want, too.

ALESANDRO'S BROKEN HEART RECOVERY PLAN

Soothe

My Favorite Soothe Skills

Forgive to move on.

Spend time with your best self.

Write it out.

Breathe slowly and deeply.

Try tincture of time.

It is what it is.

My Favorite Soothe Activities

I like to work out, so I have that. I'll wear the sweater my grandmother knitted for me. It reminds me of her and I always feel better when I wear it. I made a broken heart playlist of my favorite songs. I have a couple about surviving break-ups and they're inspiring. I'll listen to those. I'll take a few long hikes in the woods near my house. I always feel better when I'm in nature.

Support

Justin   I know I can text him any time. He's my best friend and he's always there for me. We usually work out together when we're upset about something. Maybe I'll suggest we meet at the gym when I want to talk.

Jessica   She's usually pretty busy but she's easy to reach at night. I'll just text her and then talk. She's a great listener and I usually feel the most down at night and so she's a great late-night friend.

Tony   He's a doer so he's great when I want to get my mind off things. Last time we went for a bike ride around town. It was fun and helped me get out of my head. He's funny too and that helps.

| Ms. Cole | I can hang back after English class and talk to her. She's a great listener and she might go for a walk with me at lunch like she did a few months ago. |
| Father Ramon | I can tell him at Sunday mass that I want to talk to him, or I can drop in to see him at the church youth center. |

" Bethany totally broke my heart. I know that when you meet someone there's a chance that one person will be more into the other person, so I know if you date enough then sooner or later your heart is going to get broken. But after the breakup with Bethany, it was weird how stressed and worried I felt about dating again. Creating a broken heart recovery plan helped me feel less stressed about the whole dating scene. Obviously I still never want someone to break my heart again, but knowing how to manage the pain of a broken heart makes dating again less scary and stressful.

—Alesandro **"**

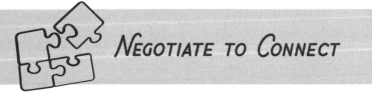

NEGOTIATE TO CONNECT

Negotiation is another great skill to cope with the stress of creating and maintaining intimate relationships. Negotiation also improves and deepens relationships, which helps you feel more secure and less stressed. Negotiating means you and the other person work to find a compromise to a situation, so that each of you wins a little and loses a little—that way, you both win. Negotiating a compromise can prevent future disagreements or conflicts about a situation because everyone involved feels like they've gotten something. Because people are different, they often have different solutions to a problem. So it's important to consider not only what you want and how you will ask for it, but also the effect of what you want and how you ask for it on the other person. Will your suggestion solve the problem or make it worse? Will making your request improve your relationship with the person or damage it? The best negotiations begin before you even meet and speak with the person. A little preparation pays big time when negotiating a compromise. Follow these steps to negotiate to connect:

1. Make a T-chart by drawing two columns on a blank piece of paper.

2. At the top of the left column, write "Where I Could Give a Little" and then write the things about the situation where you could give a little.

3. At the top of the right column, write "Where I Hold Firm" and list those things you want to stick to.

4. Then try to find a middle ground. Review the ideas in both columns and write several middle-ground ideas. These are ways you might compromise. Feel free to include any idea, even a silly one, to shift your creative mind into gear. Remember that a compromise is in the eye of the beholder. You might be surprised sometimes what middle-ground idea the other person thinks is a compromise.

5. Finally, meet face-to-face, and negotiate your compromise. Sometimes the first compromise doesn't work. Or you realize that you've given more than the other person and it doesn't feel good. If this is the case, go back to the T-chart and review your ideas. Then, let the other person know the first compromise didn't work for you and that you'd like to try again.

During the negotiation, signal to the other person that you're open and there is a middle ground. Smile, nod your head as you listen, let them know you're happy to negotiate and that you'll be fair to them and to yourself.

> **❝** I love Tim but we don't always see eye to eye. Last Saturday night we were hanging out and decided to watch a show together. I wanted to watch a romantic comedy, but Tim wanted to watch the new horror movie. I said that was a Big No! But I didn't want to argue with him about movies. I just wanted to hang out and have fun. I decided to try the negotiate to connect skill. First, I thought about where I could give a little. I decided that I'd be okay with a scary movie if it wasn't too scary. Maybe we could find a zombie rom com. Who knows? I also thought if we couldn't find a movie we both liked, I'd suggest we play Scrabble. Scrabble isn't my thing but Tim loves it. When I suggested these options to him, he surprised me and compromised. He said that if we played a couple of Scrabble games he'd watch a funny rom com with me. That worked for me.
> —Ofelia **❞**

Forgive to Move On

Your significant other stands you up, or your ex starts dating your friend. You're feeling hurt and start fuming, day and night, over and over. As you do, a slow burning grudge grows deep inside you. As long as you hold a grudge, you're stuck in hurt, in resentment, and in stress because you worry that you'll see the person, or because you keep thinking about what he said, what she did, and how upset you feel. Holding a grudge is stressful!

Believe it or not, forgiveness is the antidote to hurt, disappointment, and frustration, especially when there's nothing you can do to change the person or the situation. You might ask, if forgiveness helps us so much, why is it so difficult to do? Well, it's because most people don't understand what forgiveness is and what it is not.

What Forgiveness Is and Is Not

To forgive is to decide to let go. By forgiving, you accept what happened and find a way to live with it. Forgiveness doesn't happen overnight. It's not easy for most people. Forgiveness takes time, and, for many, it's a gradual process.

Most important, forgiveness is for you, it's not for the person who wronged you. Forgiving doesn't even need to include that person. Most times, people won't even know that you've forgiven them. In addition, forgiveness does *not* mean that:

- You must excuse the person's actions.
- You must stop feeling hurt or upset about what happened.
- You must forget what happened.
- You must tell the person that you forgive them.
- You must include the person in your life.

Four Steps of Forgiveness

Forgiveness begins with a recognition of your suffering and a willingness to make things better for yourself. Forgiveness is an ongoing action you take in response to feelings of resentment, disappointment, and anger toward another person. Forgiveness is hard, but constantly holding on to resentment and disappointment is hard too! To forgive to move on, find a quiet and comfortable place to be alone with your thoughts and follow these steps:

1. **Acknowledge the event and how it affected you.** Think about the event that hurt you. Open yourself to the hurt and accept how you feel about the event and the person who hurt you. Remind yourself that you may not get what you want even though you are a good person. Acknowledge that you might, in fact, get something better or worse than what you want. For example, you might acknowledge in this way, "Even though I wanted Gloria to like me, I understand and accept that she might not like me and that doesn't make me or her a bad person."

2. **Acknowledge that with every hurt there is something for you to learn if you are open to learning it.** What did you learn about yourself that can help you grow from the event? Is this new knowledge useful to you? Is the lesson learned worth the hurt if you can use this new knowledge in the future? Decide (and it is a decision) to reconnect with your big dreams and your deepest hopes. Acknowledge that the hurt is part of your growth and development as a person. For example, you might acknowledge in this way, "I have learned to be a better friend and this new knowledge will help me be a better friend to my other friends."

3. **Acknowledge that the person is flawed and imperfect because all human beings are flawed and imperfect.** Consider that the person may have acted without understanding the effects on you, or from the belief that their actions are okay or that the circumstance makes the action okay. Remind yourself that at times we all act from our limited understanding. Perhaps the person hurt you because they needed something from you or from someone else. What do you think the person needed? Why did they go after what they needed in a way that hurt you? For example, you might acknowledge in this way, "Gloria is unable to see the good in me. This is her limitation."

4. **Acknowledge the importance of practicing forgiveness every day.** Remind yourself that forgiveness is a process and that each day presents opportunities to practice forgiveness, with this hurt and with the next one. Since you may slip back into your old pattern of holding a grudge, ask a trusted friend or family member to remind you to forgive. Find people who have successfully forgiven others and listen

to what they have to say. At times, you won't be able to set aside the hurt and resentment. Go ahead and give yourself permission to mull over the grudge for a short period—perhaps 15 minutes—then move on with your life. For example, you might acknowledge in this way, "I decided today to learn all that I can to heal from this hurt and to move ahead with my life."

66 I really like Anya but sometimes she can say mean things. Last week, she called me a jerk because I was late picking her up to go to the movie. For days, all I could think about was what Anya said and how much it hurt my feelings. I just kept thinking about how unfair it was, night and day, over and over. I realized that holding on to the hurt and resentment was exhausting me, and it was stressful too. I wasn't sleeping. I wasn't eating. I just kept thinking about what Anya said, and it wasn't changing anything. She said what she said. My buddies tell me that she probably isn't even thinking about any of this. Today, I decided that I would start to forgive. I know it'll take some time, but I'm already feeling lighter. I can tell that I'm starting to move on.
—Deion 99

TRY TINCTURE OF TIME

Time is the best healer. It's a cliché, but it's true! Many times, when something upsets or stresses you, it feels like the most important thing in the world. But transporting yourself into the future and then looking back at the event can help you feel better. Whatever seemed important when it happened can feel less important after some time has passed. For example, when your significant other doesn't return your texts, you might feel intensely upset, stressed, or even angry because this event feels very important in the moment. But at the end of the week, one day without texts from your significant other will seem less important. That's when you'll notice that you feel less stressed and hurt. Tincture of time works well for other feelings too, such as guilt, embarrassment, or even anger. Follow these steps to try tincture of time:

1. At the top of a blank sheet of paper, describe the event that upset you.

2. Rate how important the event feels now. Use a 0 to 5 importance scale, where 0 means that *it's not at all important*, 3 means that *it's important but not life changing*, and 5 means that your *life depends on it*.

3. Rate how important the event will feel in an hour and then a day, then a week, month, year, 5 years, and 10 years.

4. Re-rate how important the event feels after you completed the exercise. That's tincture of time!

Look at Ofelia's *Try Tincture of Time Exercise* to get an idea of how to she did this, and then you try it.

OFELIA'S TRY TINCTURE OF TIME EXERCISE

Event that Upset You

We were hanging out with Tim's friends and he pushed me away a little when I tried to give him a kiss.

*Rate how important (0 to 5) this event feels **at the moment**:* 5

Ask yourself the following questions and re-rate the importance (0 to 5) each time:

How important will this event feel in an hour? 5

How important will this event feel in a day? 4

How important will this event feel in a week? 3

How important will this event fell in a month? 1

How important will this event feel in a year? 0

How important will this event feel in 5 years? 0

How important will this event feel in 10 years? 0

*Re-rate how important this event feels **now**:* 1

➯ TRY IT HERE TOO: Tincture of time helps with almost any situation. Time doesn't care whether it's a breakup, a poor grade on a test, an argument with a friend, or an embarrassing moment. Tincture of time helps with any hard knock of life. Try it next time you trip in front of a crowd or a new friend ghosts you for a few days.

☼ STRESS HACK: Stress and anxiety are all about something bad that could happen that isn't happening right now. When you're stressed or anxious, it can help to remind yourself that in this moment, you're okay. Several times a day, notice that you're okay. If you're worried that you'll get a bad grade on the test tomorrow and lower your GPA, but right now your GPA is okay, say softly to yourself "*Right now, I'm okay.*" If you're stressed that your significant other might breakup with you tomorrow, but right now you're still together, say softly to yourself "*Right now, I'm okay.*" Even if something bad did happen, say softly to yourself "*Right now, I'm okay.*" because deep down, regardless of what happened, you're okay.

❝ When I heard that Boyd invited Betsy to the prom instead of me, I couldn't believe it. I thought for certain he was into me. I was stressing about it all night long. Then I remembered the Tincture of Time skill. At first, this felt like the most important thing in my life but then, as I transported myself to the future and looked back at it over days and months, it felt less important. That's when I started to feel less hurt and stressed. By the time I asked myself how important this would be in a year, I realized I probably wouldn't care at all. I tried the Tincture of Time skill with embarrassment too and it worked great. The other day, I dropped my tray in the cafeteria. I thought I was going to die of embarrassment. I used the Tincture of Time skill, and realized in a year I probably wouldn't even remember it. I didn't think about dropping the tray all night, and the next day I ate in the cafeteria and barely thought about it.

—Lois

"

STRESS HACK: When people feel stressed, they often try to get the stressful thoughts out of their minds. This never works, but what can work is a little perspective. There's no better way to create perspective than humor. If you ever took an improv comedy class, you likely learned *Yes, and* . . . . In *Yes, and* . . . you accept whatever the other person in the scene says and you add something more. You don't disagree, contradict, or shut down the other person. You accept it and build on it. This strategy is a great way to add perspective to a stressful thought or worry. For example, to the stressful thought, "*What if I fail the pop quiz?*" you might add, "*Yes, and then I'll fail high school, can't go to college, my family rejects me, and I live in a van down by the river.*" Or, to the worry, "*What if the bruise on my hand means I have a fatal disease?*" you might add, "*Yes, and it's time to call the funeral home to schedule my memorial service.*" The point of *Yes, and* . . . is to exaggerate the worry so that it seems less important to you. You'll get a chuckle out of it too!

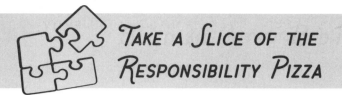

TAKE A SLICE OF THE RESPONSIBILITY PIZZA

Almost nothing is just one person's fault. Life is more complicated than that. Life is messy and responsibility, like a pizza, can be divided into many slices. Even when it feels like all the responsibility is yours, you really have just one slice among many! Sharing the responsibility can help you feel less stressed and upset at yourself. Rather than blaming yourself completely and totally when something doesn't work out, step back and divide up the whole pizza into individual slices. Redistributing responsibility redistributes blame, if you want to call it that. Taking your share and only your share, and giving other people or events their share, can very quickly help you feel less stressed and upset. Follow these steps to Take a Slice of the Responsibility Pizza:

1. Describe a recent upsetting event and why you think it's your fault.

2. Rate how strongly you believe (0 to 100%, where 100% means you believe it completely) that the event is your fault. Then rate how stressed or upset you feel (0 to 10, where 10 is extreme).

3. List as many other factors that may have contributed to the upsetting event that you can think of (factors can be other people, too).

4. Review the list and assign each factor a percent for how much you think it contributed to the event.

5. Include yourself as the final factor and assign yourself a percentage amount.

6. Review all the factors and their percentage of responsibility. Compare this to your percentage. Be sure the total percentage across all the factors you listed adds up to 100%.

7. Re-rate how strongly you believe that the event is your fault. Then rate how stressed or upset you feel.

Look at Kanesha's *Take A Slice of the Responsibility Pizza Exercise* to see how she did this.

KANESHA'S TAKE A SLICE OF THE RESPONSIBILITY PIZZA EXERCISE

Upsetting Event: Trevor broke up with me because sometimes I argued with him.

How strongly do you believe that the upsetting event is your fault?   90%

How stressed or upset do you feel now?   9

Other factors that may have contributed to event

Trevor has been unhappy about a lot of stuff, not just our relationship: 10%

Me: 5%

Lisa has been talking trash about me to Trevor: 5%

Trevor is stressed about his college applications: 10%

Trevor is going through a lot because of his parents' divorce: 50%

His parents fight all the time and that upsets him: 20%

Now, how strongly do you believe that the upsetting event is your fault?   20%

Now, how stressed or upset do you feel?   3

66 I was totally stressed and upset after Trevor broke up with me. It felt like it was totally my fault because he and I argued so much. But when I looked at all the slices of the responsibility pizza, I realized that it definitely wasn't all my fault that we broke up. It wasn't all Trevor's fault either. There were a lot of things that neither of us could control. They just happened. Now, I realize that several things usually cause something to happen, and a lot of them are out of my control. There's no reason to feel so stressed and upset about my little slice of pizza. **99**
—Kanesha

⇄ TRY IT HERE TOO: The *Take a Slice of the Responsibility Pizza* is a great skill to use when you're blaming someone else (not yourself) for something that happened in life, too. Sometimes it's easier to blame someone else for what happened than it is to accept your slice of the responsibility pizza. Yes, it may be a very small slice, but it's still a slice. But holding a grudge is stressful. Furthermore, blaming other people doesn't resolve conflict. It only increases the likelihood that you'll get angry and make things worse for yourself. Then things get really stressful for you. If you want to feel less angry and stressed so that you can move on, try slicing the responsibility pizza. It works the same way, except you start with the other person's responsibility rather than yours, and then you brainstorm all the factors, including you, that may have also contributed to the event that upset you.

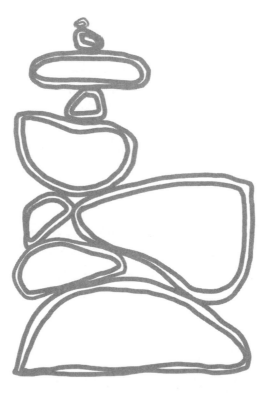

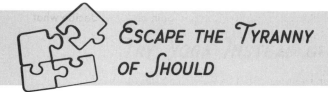

Escape the Tyranny of Should

"Should" statements can increase your stress and worry because thinking you "should" or "have to" or "need to" do something increases the pressure you feel to do it: "I should drop everything any time my partner wants to talk. I should always be nice to my boyfriend even if he does something that bothers me." Also, thinking that you "should have" done something can cause you to feel needlessly guilty and bad about yourself: "I should have been nicer to my girlfriend," or, "I should have known better."

This way of thinking is called the "Tyranny of Should." But why is all the "should" thinking a tyranny? Think back to history class. Remember all those tyrants: Henry the Eighth, Attila the Hun, Genghis Khan? They told people what to do and they did it or else. People who lived under the rule of a tyrant didn't have a choice. That's what it's like when you live under the "should" tyrant. When you do something just because you think you should, you serve the "should" tyrant. Life in a tyranny is hard because it feels like you don't have much choice or free will. People who live under the Tyranny of Should feel more stressed, more anxious, more guilty, and more down. But when you take charge of your choices, you take charge of your life. That's when you'll start to feel empowered, in charge, less stressed, and happier. To escape the tyranny of should, follow these steps:

1. On the top of a blank sheet of paper, write a should that's causing you to feel stressed or upset. The should might be about the kind of romantic partner that you believe you "should" be, or what you "should" or "shouldn't" do on that first date.

2. Next, draw a line down the center of the page. Label the left column "What I lose" and the right column "What I gain."

3. In each column, write the things that you might lose or gain if you do what the tyrant is telling you that you should (or shouldn't) do.

4. Step back and look at what you lose and gain and then decide what you want to do and why. Write this at the bottom of the page as a preference, wish, or desire.

Asif tried this when he noticed that he was telling himself that he "should" pretend that he's interested in what Leo, a guy he likes, is saying rather than telling him things that he likes to do.

ASIF'S ESCAPE THE TYRANNY OF SHOULD EXERCISE

Should that you wish to escape:

I should pretend that I'm interested in what Leo is saying, when I'm not.

What I lose:	What I gain:
I like Leo and want to enjoy my time with him. Listening to him talk about stuff that I have zero interest in isn't fun for me and makes me not want to hang out with him.	Leo enjoys talking about the stuff he likes. If I pretend to be interested in what he says, then he'll want to see me more.
If I want Leo to get to know me better, and I do, then not telling him what I'm into doesn't build our relationship.	If I don't tell Leo about the things that interest me, he won't dislike me.
Time! I've got a ton of homework to do. I'm willing to spend time with Leo but not like this.	I'd like to date Leo and the time is worth it, if I'm enjoying myself.

Re-state as a desire, wish or want:

I want to share what I like and what I'm doing with Leo so that I enjoy myself and build a friendship that might lead to something more. Who knows?

TRY IT HERE TOO: The tyranny of should can create stress in other areas of your life too, not just in your intimate relationships and dating. "I should always get As," "I should always be nice to my friends," "I should never make a mistake on a test, in a game, or when playing the piano." Yes, the tyranny of should can make almost every area of your life harder, if you let it. Use the Escape the Tyranny of Should skill to tackle these "shoulds" too.

STRESS HACK: Most people are unaware of the number of times they think or say the word "should" or the shoulds-in-sheep's-clothing—"must," "have to," "got to," "ought to," and "need to." This way of thinking might be second nature to you. You think them and say them automatically. An easy way to break this pattern is to count the "shoulds." For a week or two, place pennies in one pocket and transfer a penny to the other pocket each time you think or say "should" and then place the "should" pennies (or other tokens if you're short of pennies) in a jar so that you can see the full weight of the tyranny under which you live. Or you can mark on a piece of paper each time you think or say "should." As you become more aware of how often your "shoulds" push you around, you'll find it easier to let go of them.

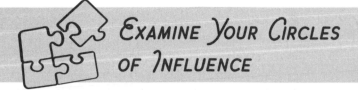

Examine Your Circles of Influence

Stress or anxiety motivates us to take charge of a situation, if we can, and influence the potential threat we face. However, influence isn't the same as control. Control, or 100% influence, is a myth. A comforting myth, but a myth nonetheless. In reality, we have different degrees of influence over events and situations, but rarely 100% influence. For example, if you're stressed about an upcoming first date, you might take charge of the situation by finding out a little more about the person by talking to a friend who knows the person well, or taking special care choosing what you'll wear, or asking your mom for first-date tips. In other words, you have a high degree of influence over your actions. These actions likely influence how well you do on the first date. Similarly, you have a high degree of influence over how you think about the first date. If you think that you're going to make a fool of yourself, you'll probably feel very stressed and may not share much about yourself, or you may even cancel the date. That's no way to meet the person of your dreams!

But what influence do you have over what your friend knows and doesn't know about the person, or about the person's tastes in clothing, or whether your mom's first-date tips still work in the 21st century? Not much! In fact, focusing on aspects of problems or situations over which you have little or no influence will only cause you to feel needless stress, worry, and sometimes panic.

In order to feel less stressed, helpless, and out of control, focus your attention and actions on areas you have the greatest influence over. To get an idea of how to do this, think in terms circles of influence:

- **No influence circle:** This includes the wide range of circumstances or problems over which you have no influence. This includes problems you can't do anything about because they're done and in the past, such as changing how well the date went last Saturday, or the tastes or opinions of other people, such as whether you and your first date share the same taste in music. The no influence circle is the largest circle because there are so many things that we have no influence over.

- **Medium influence circle:** This includes circumstances or problems that we have some but limited influence over. This includes problems involving the behaviors of other people, such as your partner who is chronically late. You can't directly control your partner, but there's a good chance that you can influence their actions by your own actions and choices. For example, you can speak to your chronically late partner and ask them to try to arrive on time, or if your partner simply cannot arrive on time, plan how you'll use your time while you wait.

- **High influence circle:** This includes those circumstances or problems that you have very high and direct influence over. Perhaps what you have the highest influence over is the way that you think and act. Even then, you don't have 100% influence over whether particular thoughts come into your mind or not. You can, however, decide whether or not to believe the thought, dwell on the thought, or act on the thought. For example, you have a high degree of influence over whether you continue to date the person or even whether you go out with them when they're late to pick you up. You also have a high degree of influence over how much you care about your partner's tardiness.

CIRCLES OF INFLUENCE

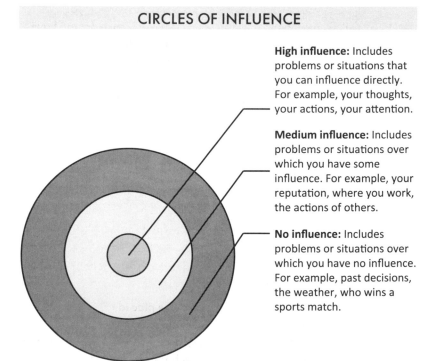

High influence: Includes problems or situations that you can influence directly. For example, your thoughts, your actions, your attention.

Medium influence: Includes problems or situations over which you have some influence. For example, your reputation, where you work, the actions of others.

No influence: Includes problems or situations over which you have no influence. For example, past decisions, the weather, who wins a sports match.

If you tend to focus on aspects of problems or situations over which you have very little or no influence at all, it's a formula for stress and worry, not to mention it's a huge waste of your time and energy. Focusing, instead, on aspects of problems or situations over which you have the greatest influence will help you feel less stressed, worried, and more in control of your life. To examine your circles of influence, follow these steps:

1. On a blank sheet of paper, draw the circles of influence.

2. Cut sticky notes into strips. On each strip, write an issue, problem or situation that is bothering you or stressing you out about dating or your intimate relationship. Place the sticky strips along the top of the page.

3. Think about each problem or situation and ask yourself how much influence you have over it. For example, how much influence do you have over whether the first date goes well, and how would you influence the outcome of the date, if you could? You could ask the person questions to learn more about their likes or dislikes, or you could suggest a place you like that's fun for the first date, or you could remind yourself that whether it's a great date or not, you can try to make a new friend. Similarly, how much influence do you have over whether your partner is grouchy or not, and how might you think about this or what might you do to influence your partner's grouchiness? You could ask your partner (nicely) why they seem upset recently and see if there is something you could do to help, or you could limit the time you spend with your partner when they're grouchy, or when your partner is grouchy, you could include other fun non-grouchy friends to make it more fun for you.

4. As you think through the degree and form of influence you have over each problem or situation, move the strips from the top of the page and into one of the circles of influence. As you think through your influence over the problems, you might find that some of the concerns go straight into the circle of no influence. This may mean that you can only influence how you think about the problem, or whether to dwell on the problem or let it go.

5. When you're comfortable with where you've placed the sticky strips of paper in the three circles of influence, place the sheet of paper in a place where you can easily see it every day. If you don't want anyone to see it, place the sheet of paper on the back of your bedroom closet door or inside your school locker. That way, you'll remember how much influence you have over the problems and situations that are stressing you, and this will help you focus your time and energy on managing the things that you can.

⇄ TRY IT HERE TOO: Try the *Examine Your Circles of Influence Exercise* with athletic or artistic performances, taking tests, upcoming events, or even a friend who is often grouchy with you. Write on the strips of sticky paper what you have no influence, medium influence, and high influence over. If you're stressed about an upcoming soccer game, you might write, *Calls the referee makes* on a sticky strip and place this in the no influence circle (although you could speak to the referee about a bad call . . . good luck with that!). You might write, *My energy level* on a sticky strip and place this in the medium circle of influence. You can try to get to bed early, eat well, and stretch before the game—but sometimes things get in the way of a good night's sleep. Or you might write, *My game head* on a sticky strip. After all, you have the most influence, pretty close to 100%, on what you'll think about before and during the game. Will you think about how you'll recover from a mistake rather than dreading making one? Will you think positively about the game and share that attitude with your teammates? Will you focus on the ball or on the score? Place the sticky strips in the circles of influence and place the paper where you can see it prior to the game or performance.

❝ I tried the Examine Your Circles of Influence Exercise and it helped me get a grip on the dating scene. I don't have control over whether a date goes well or not. I can only do my part and that's helped me feel less stressed and worried about meeting new people and going on first dates. I had no idea how much I focused on things that I had no influence over. Before a date, I worry about whether the person likes the shoes I wear. What influence do I have over someone else's taste in shoes? Or, when it comes to my basketball game, I'm thinking about how my teammates will play; or, what calls the referees will make. What a waste of time. I realized what I have the most influence over is what I do and how I think. The rest only stresses me out!

—Asif **❞**

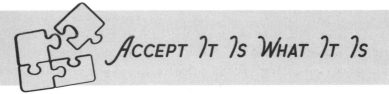

Accept It Is What It Is

When someone you love or care about hurts you, your first reaction might be to fight your feelings and the situation. You might blame the person or yourself for how you feel. You might dwell on the past event as you repeatedly ask yourself why it happened: why did he do that, why did she say that. This only distracts you from the fact that it did happen and that the only thing you can do is to deal with it. Fighting the distress only intensifies and prolongs your pain and suffering. Clearly, this attitude doesn't work—not for you and not for anyone.

A different attitude can help you suffer less. It's the *It Is What It Is* attitude, and it's both radical and counter-intuitive: accepting rather than fighting stress and distress is the key to feeling less stress and distress.

It Is What It Is Replaces Powerlessness with Power

It Is What It Is recognizes that the only influence you have is in the present moment. It means that by accepting the situation, you stop trying to change something that you can't, which frees you to focus on what you *can* do now. There is nothing you can do to change the past. No amount of anger, resentment, hurt, or stress will change what happened. No amount of thinking about the past event will change the event now. In fact, when you focus on the past—what they said, the breakup, the hurt, the stress—you're stuck in the past. *It Is What It Is* lessens your distress because as you focus on the here and now you have greater influence over how you feel in the moment and what you can do in that moment and in the next one. But taking an *It Is What It Is* attitude doesn't mean that what your significant other did, or what happened on the first date was okay. It just means that you accept that what is done is done, whether it was right or wrong, good or bad.

It Is What It Is Provides Perspective

It Is What It Is recognizes that the present situation exists as a result of a long series of events that began far in the past, like a line of dominoes. One domino knocks over the next domino, and so on. For example, your boyfriend broke up with you because he was unhappy. He was unhappy because his parents divorced. His parents divorced because they argued with each other. They argued with each other because your boyfriend's father was unhappy. Your boyfriend's father was unhappy because he lost his job. He lost his job because the factory shut down. The factory shut down because people wanted a cheaper widget from overseas. Now if you change any one of these links in the chain of events you might change the final event that is causing you to feel how you're feeling now. But which event? Even if you knew which event, could you have changed it? And most importantly, can you change any of these events now? Almost certainly not. *It Is What It Is* lessens your distress because you can see that you and your actions are a small cog in the enormous machine called life.

How to Practice It Is What It Is

To practice *It Is What It Is*, imagine a past distressing event or situation. It could be any upsetting moment from the past. For example, the moment your boyfriend broke up with you, or the moment the person stood you up, or the moment your best friend started to date your ex. Now, answer the following questions:

- What happened in this distressing situation?

- What past events led to this situation?

- What role did I play in this situation?

- What roles did other people play in creating this situation?

- What do I have influence over in this situation?

- What don't I have influence over in this situation?

- What were my thoughts and feelings to the situation?

- How did my thoughts and feelings affect the thoughts and feelings of other people?

- How could I have changed my response to this situation in order to suffer less?

- How could the situation have happened differently if I had accepted the situation?

Look at Kanesha's *Accept It Is What It Is Exercise* to see how she did it. Kanesha practiced with the moment Trevor broke up with her.

KANESHA'S ACCEPT IT IS WHAT IT IS EXERCISE

What happened in this distressing situation?

Trevor told me that it wasn't a good time for him to be in a serious relationship and wanted to break up.

What past events led to this situation?

Trevor's dad left, and his mom needed him. This put a lot of pressure on Trevor. He started to miss school and flunked a couple of tests. Trevor's sister wouldn't help out and everything was on Trevor's shoulders.

What role did I play in creating this situation?

Instead of supporting Trevor, I made him feel bad about breaking up.

What roles did other people play in creating this situation?

Trevor's dad left. Trevor's mom was too dependent on Trevor. Trevor's older sister didn't help Trevor.

What do I have influence over in this situation?

I have influence over how I treat Trevor but not much else.

What don't I have influence over in this situation?

I don't influence Trevor's dad, mom, sister, or Trevor's reaction to his dad leaving.

What were my thoughts and feelings to the situation?

I was hurt and thought Trevor didn't care about me. I blamed him for the breakup.

How did my thoughts and feelings affect the thoughts and feelings of other people?

I made Trevor feel worse when I blamed him for the situation. He felt so bad that he couldn't even look at me.

How could I have changed my response to this situation in order to suffer less?

I could have seen that Trevor was having a hard time and supported his decision to take care of himself for a while. I could have accepted that I didn't like the situation but I couldn't change it either.

How could the situation have happened differently if I had accepted the situation?

If I had supported Trevor then we might have been able just to take a break from the relationship. I wouldn't have felt so hurt and angry and we could have supported each other like we usually do.

You can use *It Is What It Is* self-talk to enter this mindset. These are coping phrases that encourage you to accept the present moment exactly as it was meant to be, given all that happened before. To practice *It Is What It Is* self-talk, silently repeat these phrases to yourself. Select the phrases that feel right to you or come up with your own. Repeat the phrases to yourself next time you're feeling distressed or dwelling on a past upsetting event:

IT IS WHAT IT IS SELF-TALK

It is what it is.	This is the way it was meant to be.
Resist and persist, accept to move on.	All the events led to this moment now.
Fighting the past does not change the past.	I can't change what has happened.
This moment is what it is, even if I don't like what led to this moment.	This present moment is what it is given all that's happened before.
It's a waste of time and effort to fight what happened.	I can't control the past, I only have this moment. What will I do with it?
This present moment is the result of a million decisions and actions.	The present moment is the only moment I can influence.

" When Trevor broke up with me, I was devastated. I kept thinking that it was totally unfair. The more I thought about the breakup the worse I felt. I kept playing the scene over and over in my mind, then I started to blame myself for the breakup. I felt horrible for weeks and it didn't change anything. Then one day as I was complaining to my best friend, she put her arms around me and said, "It is what it is." That helped me snap out of it a little. That's when I started to practice the It Is What It Is skill. After a while I started to feel better. It didn't change what had happened, but somehow accepting what had happened helped me start to move on.

—Kanesha **"**

BUILD A SUPPORT NETWORK

Handling the stress of a break-up, or the stress of a relationship that isn't going well, is difficult to do on your own. Building a network of friends, family members, and other special people can help. This support network might look very similar to your heartbreak recovery support network—maybe it's exactly the same! But this support network can also be a bit more broad, and include more people who can talk about different kinds of emotions, stress, or just events of the day. To build a support network, follow these steps:

1. It's important to build a network of people who can support you in a variety of ways. In your network, include people who can support you in one of three ways.

TYPES OF SUPPORT

Emotional	Practical	Informational
These people support your emotional well-being. They're good listeners and love and care about you. They'll listen without judging you or telling you what to do.	These people have great ideas and are great problem-solvers. They're not always great listeners, but they care about you and want to help in practical ways.	These people are well connected in the community. They can tell you where to go for help or who to talk to. They know what's happening in school, in your neighborhood, or in your religious community and can provide you with great resources.

2. Think about people who love, support, and care for you. Don't forget to include people outside your friendship or family networks, such as a special teacher, coach, or spiritual leader in your community.

3. On a blank sheet of paper, list the names of the family, friends, and other people and the types of support the person can provide you. Don't forget to include organizations or activities too, like the youth group at your church, or the support group at school.

4. Next to each person, group, or organization, write the type of support they provide: *E: Emotional; P: Practical; I: Informational.*

5. Place the page with your support network in a private place and update it from time to time. Friends change. Life changes. You want your network to reflect where you are in your life.

Look at the *Support Network* Kanesha built to see how she did it.

KANESHA'S SUPPORT NETWORK

Family

	E	P	I
1. My mom, of course.	X		
2. Aunt Willie, she knows everyone.			X
3. My younger sister, she's a good listener.	X	X	
4. Jasmine, my favorite cousin.	X		

Friends

	E	P	I
1. Krystal, she's my best friend.	X		
2. Alexis, she's been through a break-up.		X	X
3. Imani, a church friend.	X		
4. Jasmine, field hockey buddy.		X	X

Others

	E	P	I
1. Reverend Thomas, he's really calm.	X	X	
2. Ms. Morris, my favorite teacher.	X	X	X
3. Mr. Reston, my coach.		X	
4. Ms. Charles, school counselor.	X	X	X

Community

	E	P	I
1. Church youth group.	X	X	X
2. Pottery club at school.	X	X	

🌰 In a Nutshell

Whether it's a first date, a breakup, or relationship drama, learning skills to deal with dating and relationship stress plays a vital role in building intimate and lasting relationships with the special people in your life. Many of the skills to manage dating and relationship stress work well with friends, teachers, or even strangers, and will help you grow and nurture these relationships too.

*C*HAPTER 7
Media and Technology Stress

Media and technology has made life easier in a lot of ways. It's simple to stay in touch with family and friends who live far away, and practically all of the information in the world is at your fingertips! But excessive media and technology use can create a great deal of stress and unhappiness, as well as make it difficult to get the sleep you need and stay on top of the many tasks on your plate. Learning skills to manage media time, as well as cope with media overload and media relationships, is vital to the success of everyone in this tech-driven world. In this chapter, you'll learn the following skills to handle media and technology stress:

- Track Your Media and Technology Use
- Manage Media and Technology Time
- Take Media and Technology Breaks
- Put Media and Technology to Bed
- Set Healthy Social Media Boundaries
- Do One Thing at a Time
- Overcome Fear of Missing Out
- Tell Your Side of the Story
- Handle Cyberbullying
- Deal with Boredom Off-Device

TRACK YOUR MEDIA AND TECHNOLOGY USE

You have the same time as everyone else—friends, teachers, parents, co-workers, the President—and it's 24 hours per day. For most people, some of that time is spent on screens. Screen time includes all screens: smart phone, laptop or desktop computer, tablet, or television. In general, you spend time on screens in three ways:

- **Required time:** Some of the screen time you can't avoid. That's screen time you use to complete homework, to check your class schedule, or even to take an online class.

- **Fun time:** Then there's *fun* time. That's screen time you use to watch television, YouTube videos, shows, or movies, to play games, or whatever else that's fun for you.

- **Social time:** Social time includes quick text exchanges with friends or family members, reading your social media feeds, or posting something. You might send a fun meme to a friend or watch a show together online. Or you might do your homework with a friend while you're both online.

The first step to manage media and technology stress is to identify the amount of time you spend on screens and what you're doing when you're on them. Although you may have an impression of how much time you spend on screens, do you really know exactly what you're doing on screens and how much time you're spending? For example, although most of the time during the week you're sitting in class, what about your screen use between classes? Are you on your phone texting or checking your social media feed as you walk to your next class? When you're hanging out with friends, are you on your phone scanning the internet for the latest news about your favorite singer or band? How much time do you spend watching reels or TikTok videos, YouTube channels, or streaming shows, and on what device? Follow these steps to track your screen time:

1. On a blank sheet of paper, draw seven vertical lines on the paper to make eight columns. At the top of the far left column, write *Time of Day*, then at the top of the next seven columns write the day of the week (Monday through Sunday).

2. Draw nineteen rows. Make each row an hour of the day, from 6:00 am to midnight.

3. Add two more rows: *Total screen use* and *Stress level*.

4. Track your total *minutes* of screen time each hour and the type of activity (**R** for required, **F** for fun, and **S** for social) and the type of screen you used (**P** for phone (or tablet), **C** for computer, **T** for television).

5. At the end of each day, calculate the total amount of time you were on a screen and rate your maximum stress level for the day from 0 to 10 (where 10 is the most stressed you can imagine feeling).

Look at Alesandro's *Media and Technology Use Exercise* to learn his screen use habits.

Your phone probably has an application that tracks your media and technology use, but it doesn't include the many other screens you use each day. So it's important to track your time and activities on all the screens you use. That way you'll have the best estimate of your media and technology use habits.

ALESANDRO'S MEDIA AND TECHNOLOGY USE EXERCISE

	Mon	Tue	Wed	Thu	Fri	Sat	Sun
6:00 am	30" S, P	30" S, P	30" S, P	30" S, P	30" S, P	Sleep	Sleep
7:00 am	30" S, P	30" S, P	30" S, P	30" S, P	30" S, P	Sleep	Sleep
8:00 am	10" S, P 30" R, C	10" S, P 30" R, C	10" S, P 30" R, C	10" S, P 30" R, C	10" S, P 30" R, C	Sleep	Sleep
9:00 am	10" S, P	10" S, P	10" S, P	10" S, P	10" S, P	Sleep	Sleep
10:00 am	10" S, P	10" S, P	10" S, P	10" S, P	10" S, P	Sleep	Sleep
11:00 am	10" S, P 30" R, C	10" S, P	10" S, P 30" R, C	10" S, P	10" S, P 30" R, C	60" S, P	60" S, P
Noon	45" S, P	45" S, P	45" S, P	45" S, P	45" S, P	30" S, P 30" F, C	60" F, T
1:00 pm	10" S, P	10" S, P	10" S, P	10" S, P	10" S, P	30" S, P 30" F, C	60" F, T
2:00 pm	10" S, P	10" S, P	10" S, P	10" S, P	10" S, P	10" S, P 30" F, C	30" S, P
3:00 pm	30" S, P	10" S, P 40" R, C	30" S, P	10" S, P 40" R, C	30" S, P	10" S, P	30" S, P 30" F, C

Time	Day 1	Day 2	Day 3	Day 4	Day 5	Day 6	Day 7
4:00 pm	50" R, C / 10" S, P	50" R, C / 10" S, P	50" R, C / 10" S, P	50" R, C / 10" S, P	30" F, C / 30" S, P	Nap	30" S, P / 30" F, C
5:00 pm	50" R, C / 10" S, P	Practice / 20" S, P	50" R, C / 10" S, P	Practice / 20" S, P	Practice / 20" S, P	Game / 20" S, P	50" R, C / 10" S, P
6:00 pm	Dinner	Dinner	Dinner	Dinner	Dinner	Game / 20" S, P	50" R, C / 10" S, P
7:00 pm	50" R, C / 10" S, P	50" R, C / 10" S, P	50" R, C / 10" S, P	50" R, C / 10" S, P	50" R, C / 10" S, P	Dinner	Dinner
8:00 pm	40" R, C / 10" S, P	50" R, C / 10" S, P	30" R, C / 30" F, P	50" R, C / 10" S, P	30" R, C / 30" F, P	50" R, C / 10" S, P	20" S, P / 40" F, T
9:00 pm	50" R, C / 10" S, P	50" R, C / 10" S, P	50" R, C / 10" S, P	30" R, C / 30" F, P	60" F, T	50" R, C / 10" S, P	60" F, T
10:00 pm	60" F, T	30" S, P	30" R, C / 30" F, P	50" R, C / 10" S, P	60" F, T	40" S, P	60" F, T
11:00 pm	60" F, T	60" F, T	60" F, T	60" F, T	60" F, T	60" F, T	10" S, P
Midnight	10" S, P	10" S, P	Sleep	10" S, P	10" S, P	60" F, T	10" S, P
Total screen use	675"	615"	675"	615"	645"	540"	680"
Stress level	4	6	5	6	6	3	4

MANAGE MEDIA
AND TECHNOLOGY TIME

Now that you have an idea of your media and technology use, the next step is to create a plan to manage it. Media and technology can save time or take time, and when it takes too much of your limited time, that means more stress for you. That's why it's important to manage your media and technology time effectively. It isn't easy, but a few small changes can free up more time to finish your work and stay more focused while you do it:

- **Delete certain apps.** If you were trying to lose a few pounds, would you do your homework with a box of donuts nearby? When you notice that a particular app is taking too much of your time, try deleting it from your phone for two weeks.

- **Move apps out of sight.** If you don't want to delete apps, try moving your high-use apps away from your phone's home screen and into folders. Out of sight is out of mind, which means that you're less likely to make that quick check of your social media feeds.

- **Use a timer to limit time.** A simple way to limit social media use is to set a timer to sound when it's okay to check social media. Then reset the timer to sound when it's time to get off social media and back to work. You can use the timer on your phone or, better yet, a kitchen timer. Although it may seem silly to use a phone app to limit social media use, there are a number of apps that can help. For example, in one app, you set a period of time (for example, 20 minutes) when you commit to not use your phone. During that time, a digital plant will grow in the app. If you use your phone during the set time, the app sends you a notification to get off your phone or your plant will die. On an iPhone, you can set Screen Time, which sets a specific amount of time you can use certain apps. Android phones have a *Digital Wellbeing* dashboard with *App Timers* that allow you to set time limits per app.

- **Turn off notifications.** Notifications constantly tempt you to check social media feeds, read the latest news article or tweet, or respond to an email. Furthermore, notifications are like someone standing behind you blowing a whistle every minute or so. It's difficult to concentrate when this is happening all day long. Try turning them off. When it's particularly important to focus, you can also turn on the *Do Not Disturb* feature, turn off data, or turn on Airplane mode.

- **Turn-off autoplay.** The auto-play feature on platforms like YouTube and Netflix is convenient, but it can also suck you into an endless stream of videos! A simple way to manage your media time is to turn off the autoplay feature. Not only will this help you manage your time, but you'll regain control over what you prefer to watch.

STRESS HACK: The colors on your devices are like candy to your brain. Change the color scheme to black and white, if you can, or muted colors that are less rewarding to your stimulation-hungry brain. Did you know that the red dots in notification messages are stressful? They alert your brain the way red traffic lights, brake lights, or stop signs do. There's a reason all those things are red!

Take Media and Technology Breaks

Media and technology occupy a huge part of everyone's life today. But sometimes it's too much. That's when it's time to take a break. The break can be as long or as short as you like, but any break can help you re-center and re-set. To take media and technology breaks, try the following:

- **Try phone-free meals.** Meals aren't just about the food. Meals are also about uninterrupted time with friends and family. Leave your phone in your bedroom during meals at home and make the most of your time with family. At lunch at school, suggest you and your friends put your phones in a pile on the table for a phone-free lunch.

- **Park your phone.** Just a little distance from the phone can help manage your media and technology time. Place your phone in your bag or backpack rather than in your pocket when hanging out with friends. You'll be less tempted by those buzzing, vibrating, and annoying reminders. When you want to take a break from social media at home, put your phone in a cupboard, drawer, or flowerpot so that you're less tempted to check it every minute.

- **Spend one hour per week on a screen-free activity.** Pick a screen-free activity and commit to spending one hour doing it once a week. Join a yoga class, read a book, plant an herb garden, or walk your dog. Develop a hobby with the time. Learn to draw, paint, or scrapbook. Try any activity that gives you a solid break from your screen. Once you enjoy spending time on the activity, increase the time, or branch out and add new activities.

Remember, small steps over time can make a big difference. It's not realistic, nor necessary, to go cold turkey. If you usually spend two hours a day on social media, try decreasing your time by ten minutes each day for two weeks. Small changes like this can generate more time, less stress, and even some fun.

-🔅- *STRESS HACK:* These days, reaching for your smartphone is automatic. It's like your phone is an extension of your hand. This makes it difficult to take a break, even a quick one, when you wish. Here are a couple of ideas to help you hit the pause button on phone use:

- Place a rubber band or hair scrunchie around your phone. The rubber band reminds you to be thoughtful and intentional when you pick up your phone.

- Modify your lock screen with a picture or an inspirational quote that reminds you to use your phone with purpose rather than as something to do when you're feeling stressed, anxious, or bored.

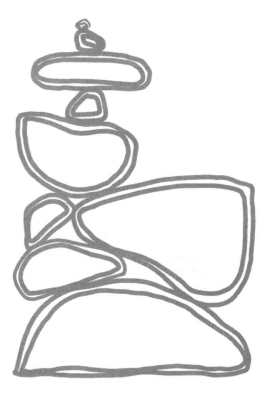

Put Media and Technology to Bed

Believe it or not, there's part of your brain that's listening to your phone, even when you're asleep. Even when your phone is in silent mode, there's a part of your brain that has been conditioned to be alert, awake, and on guard for signals from that little device. This can make it difficult for you to get all the deep, refreshing sleep your growing mind and body need. You can re-train your brain, however, if you're willing to try the following for two weeks:

- **About one hour before bed, place your phone outside your bedroom.** If you charge your phone through the night, place the charger outside your bedroom. Unless you're a brain surgeon, it's not likely that you'll receive important messages that can't wait until the morning.

- **If you use your phone to wake you in the morning, buy a real alarm clock.** If you use your phone to generate white noise, use a fan or listen to music at a low volume on a radio. Some radios have a white noise function too.

You might want to tell your friends about this experiment, particularly if they're used to you responding to every text, no matter how unimportant or late in the evening it arrives. Or, better yet, ask them to do the experiment with you.

> **Stress Hack:** Many people use their phones to entertain them in the hours before bed. Try to break this habit by finding sleep-friendly activities that are just as entertaining. Read a real book or magazine instead of reading articles on your phone. Or use an e-reader switched to the non-blue light mode.

> **"** I decided to try putting my phone outside my bedroom at bedtime. I set up a charging station in the kitchen. My little sister made a little bed for it from a shoe box with a napkin for a cover. That made me laugh. I gave it two weeks and it did seem to retrain my brain. I didn't listen for the vibrations and pings like I used to, and I think I'm sleeping a little better. My parents started to leave their phones outside their bedroom too. Now, all our phones sleep the night away in their shoebox beds. In the morning, I sometimes hear my mom and dad say "good morning" to the phones.
> —Ofelia **"**

-🔅- *STRESS HACK:* Media and technology were supposed to make your life easier, and they do when you can manage the information that constantly flows into your life. Like a computer, you can process only so much data or information at any time. Here are two simple tips to manage information overload. *First,* manage email. Ruthlessly eliminate all the non-relevant stuff that sits in your inbox. Too many emails distract you from the important ones. Flag truly important emails and respond within 24 hours. Otherwise, delete them because these "I'll reply later" emails aren't important enough to sit in your inbox. *Second,* manage subscriptions. Subscription feeds bring a relentless flow of information. It's easy to hit the subscribe button when you see an interesting blogger or podcaster, but why keep a gazillion blogs or podcasts when you won't read or listen to most of them? Limit the number of feeds to which you subscribe to six that you truly love.

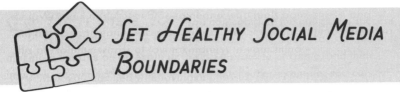

SET HEALTHY SOCIAL MEDIA BOUNDARIES

Technology has made it so we can all communicate nearly instantaneously. This is super convenient, but sometimes it means it's hard to set boundaries. It's normal for friends to talk to each other about issues with parents, peers, a teacher, or a difficult situation. But with current technology, you may be getting too much of it. At times, you may feel like a therapist because so many friends are reaching out to you for help. Or, you may have friends reaching out to you at all hours of the day and night. Although it's wonderful to help people, situations can escalate quickly and before you know it, you're in over your head.

Setting healthy boundaries means learning when to listen to a friend, and when to step back and encourage the friend to speak with a trusted adult, such as a teacher or a mental health counselor. Sometimes the most important thing you can do is to encourage a friend to speak to a trained therapist. And sometimes this means limiting your own availability, for both your sakes.

UNHEALTHY AND HEALTHY SOCIAL MEDIA BOUNDARIES

Unhealthy Boundary	Healthy Boundary
Tell friends that you're available 24 hours a day, seven days a week.	Tell friends that you're available when they're in need, but you're not available 24/7.
Leave devices and feeds on 24 hours a day so that you're available at all times.	Turn off social media and other devices in the evening or when you want a break.
Carry responsibilities alone even when you're feeling overwhelmed and overburdened.	Tell parents that you feel overwhelmed and overburdened by the needs of your friends.
Tell friends that you alone can help them and that adults wouldn't understand.	Tell friends to speak to a trusted adult in addition to you.

Respond to messages immediately regardless of the time of day or what you're doing.	Don't respond to messages at bedtime, and ask them to reach out to others if they need to speak to someone late at night.
Accept decision of friends to speak only to you and not to a therapist regardless of the seriousness of problem.	Tell friends to speak to a therapist and tell them when you feel in over your head.
Continue to help even when you're feeling overwhelmed by their problems and the responsibilities you feel.	Tell friends when you're feeling overwhelmed by their problems and want to take a break.

Now, over the next two weeks, try setting healthy boundaries to see what that's like for you. Did you feel less overwhelmed and overburdened? Did you feel less stressed and anxious? Did your friends reach out to others for help as you set healthy boundaries?

-☼- STRESS HACK: Sometimes it's difficult to set healthy boundaries, even when you know it's the right thing to do. You don't want to seem like you're not interested in helping your friends! Here are two tips to make this a little easier. *First*, when you're listening to a friend talk about a problem, picture an invisible shield around yourself. Love and caring feelings can go through the shield to your friend, but your friend's distress and problems bounce off. *Second*, imagine a way to leave your friend's distress and problems behind. For example, when you end a chat or text with a friend, visualize transferring responsibility to your friend's parents or much-loved pet; or, when walking home from hanging out with a distressed friend, identify a house, a stop sign, or a tree that is the boundary between your life and your friend's life. Then, visualize yourself walking through a force field that separates your life from your friend's life.

Do One Thing at a Time

There's an old Russian proverb that says, "If you chase two rabbits, you'll catch neither one." Your brain loves stimulation, and doing more than one thing at a time feeds that stimulation-hungry brain of yours. Unfortunately, media and technology make it easy, very easy, to do more than one thing at a time, or multitask. However, when you think you're multitasking, you aren't really. It's impossible for your brain to focus on two tasks at once. It actually rapidly switches between them. Instead of channeling your complete focus and energy into one task, you spread it thin, which prevents you from diving deep into any one of the tasks. Doing one thing at a time, rather than doing multiple things at a time, has three powerful benefits:

- **Productivity.** Doing one thing at a time is a surprisingly powerful way to become more productive. On the surface, this makes zero sense. Isn't doing more than one thing at a time the definition of productive? No, doing more than one thing at a time is the definition of busy, but it's not necessarily the definition of *productive*. When you try to do more than one task at a time, the result is that both tasks take a bit longer to complete. Not only that, when you try to do more than one thing at a time, you switch into autopilot mode, which lessens your ability to remember what you work on. That's why, when you watch a TV show while scrolling through your social media feeds, you remember less about the show. Doing one thing at a time helps you dive deeper into what you're doing and do a better job at it because you're not spreading your time, attention, and energy—the three ingredients of productivity—across too many things at once.

- **Presence.** Doing one thing at a time is more rewarding because you dive more deeply in the experience you're having in the moment. When you do one thing at a time, you're more fully present and immersed in that thing. You'll think deeper, make more connections, work more creatively, and find more meaning in everything you do because you're fully present. Whether that's eating a perfectly ripe peach or connecting with friends: you'll enjoy each activity more when you set aside your device to be fully present in the experience.

- **Pleasure.** When you make a conscious decision to do one thing at a time, you'll find more pleasure in the simplest activities. When you eat without your phone, you'll enjoy eating more. When you hang out with friends without your phone, you'll have more fun with the friends in front of you. You'll discover pleasure in menial tasks too, such as walking the dog, when you do that and only that. When you do one thing at a time, your mind can expand and creative juices flow because it's easier to be creative when you're not interrupted. When you draw or paint without your device, you'll enjoy these experiences more because you're fully immersed in that single experience and only that experience.

Doing one thing at a time is better in almost every way. However, your brain may initially resist doing one thing at a time because, well, it's less stimulating. But with practice, you'll experience greater productivity, greater presence, and greater pleasure in all the things you do. To practice doing one thing at a time, follow these steps:

1. On a blank sheet of paper, draw three vertical lines to make four columns (or you can use a blank page from a calendar). Write the days of the week (Sunday through Saturday) in the leftmost column. Then, at the top of the next three columns write: Productivity, Presence, Pleasure.

2. Once each day, for two weeks, do an activity that you usually do while you're also on your phone or other device, but this time turn off the phone or device and put it away.

3. Describe what doing one thing at a time was like for you in one or more of the three categories: Productivity, Presence, Pleasure.

Look at Asif's *Do One Thing at a Time Exercise* to see what that was like for him.

ASIF'S DO ONE THING AT A TIME EXERCISE

	Activity	Productivity	Presence	Pleasure
Sunday	Ate breakfast with five senses and no phone.		I really paid attention to the taste of the pear.	The pear I ate was incredible.
Monday	Did math homework with phone off.	I got more done and more quickly.	I concentrated better, which helped.	
Tuesday	Walked our dog without phone.		I never noticed all the birds along the path before.	I enjoyed the walk more.
Wednesday	Wrote essay with phone and computer notifications off.	I finished my essay much faster.	The ideas came faster and were better.	
Thursday	Talked to friends at lunch and kept phone in pocket.		I never noticed how funny my friends are.	It was more fun without the phone.
Friday	Rode bus home with phone in my backpack		I talked with some kids that I never noticed before.	The ride home seemed faster and more fun.
Saturday	Watched TV without phone.		I never noticed how incredible the car chase scenes are in this show.	My mom and I talked some while we watched the show together, which was great.

-☀- *STRESS HACK:* Doing one thing at a time in short bursts is a great way to get things done. Here's how to do it. Turn off and remove from your environment (if you can) all technology distractions and work on only one thing for 25 minutes. Then, take a five-minute break, and repeat (another 25 minute work burst, then a five-minute break) and repeat. After that, work for another 25 minutes and take a 15-minute break. You've earned a longer break after a focused and productive hour or more of work. How was it?

> " I never realized how often I'm on my phone while I'm doing something. It's automatic. I almost never do only one thing at a time anymore. I check my Instagram while I eat breakfast. I respond to texts when I'm on the bus talking to friends. I listen to music while I walk our dog. I decided to try doing one thing at a time for a couple of weeks. When I walked our dog, I paid attention to the walk and what I saw, heard, smelled, and felt. I enjoyed myself more and felt less stressed. It's not like I stopped using my phone, but I decided to just be on my phone when I used it. Not while I ate, or talked to friends, or watched a show with my mom. Just one thing at a time. Period!
> —Lois "

Overcome Fear of Missing Out

Fear of missing out (or FOMO) is the view that other people are having more fun, doing more interesting things, and living better lives than you are. Likely every person experiences FOMO from time to time, but social media has amplified this experience. It's easy to scroll through social media feeds and compare your life to the highlights of the lives of other people: big cars, expensive homes, amazing vacations, more friends, you name it.

Although FOMO fuels stress and anxiety, its source is a nagging unhappiness and dissatisfaction with life. Gratitude is a powerful antidote to FOMO because through gratitude you fill your life with joy and meaning. A great way to spend time with gratitude is to keep a gratitude journal. Writing down the things for which you're grateful builds the connection between those things and your emotional self. The goal of spending more time with gratitude is to remember a good event, experience, person, or thing in your life—then enjoy the good emotions that come with it. Here's how to keep a gratitude journal:

- Three times each week, write up to five things for which you feel grateful. Don't list these things in your head. It's very important that you *write* these in a journal or on a notepad. Writing builds the connection between the things and your emotional self. Your gratitude journal might include relatively big things, such as "We won the soccer championship." But it's important to write small things you're grateful for too (for example, "The chocolate chip cookie I had at lunch today"). In fact, it's likely more important to write the small things, because they happen more often, and these are the things we tend to ignore. The goal of the exercise is to remember a good thing in your life and then enjoy the good emotions that come with it.

- Try to be as specific as possible. The more specific your description, the more likely you'll take in the gratitude. For example, "I'm grateful that Luke shared half his PBJ sandwich with me today," is better than "I'm grateful Luke gave me something to eat today."

- It's better to describe something you're grateful for in detail than it is to quickly list many things without much detail. For example, "During the wind sprints at soccer practice, I'm grateful for the strength of my legs, lungs, and heart," rather than, "I'm grateful I can run."

- It's better to focus on people you're grateful for rather than on objects you're grateful for. The kindness, caring, and compassion people show you is far more important than a second helping of mashed potatoes at dinner.

- List the negative outcomes you avoided, escaped, prevented, or turned into something positive. You can be grateful for these too. This way you don't take good fortune for granted. For example, "I'm grateful that I only sprained my ankle at practice. It could've been worse!"

- See good things that come to you as "gifts." Seeing them as gifts will encourage you to appreciate them more.

- Record events that were unexpected or surprised you. You're likely to feel more grateful for unexpected gifts and good fortunes, in part, because they're above what usually comes to you. For example, "I'm grateful that Jasmine showed up at my party. I thought she was out of town."

- Write regularly. Whether you write every other day or once a week, commit to a regular time to journal, then honor that commitment.

STRESS HACK: Complaining is the opposite of gratitude. Try going on a vacation from complaining. For 30 days try not to complain about your hair, your friends, the grade on a quiz, or anything else. This doesn't mean that you have to actually think your life is perfect. It's a fact that there are things about your life that you don't like. Just try not to complain about them. It's like the old saying, "If you can't say something nice, don't say anything at all." A vacation from complaining focuses you on the good—even if it's a microscopic good—that's in almost everything. You might surprise yourself when you realize how focusing on the good improves your mood, your happiness, and your energy.

> **66** I admit it. I have a bad case of FOMO. At first, seeing the picture-perfect lives of my friends was fun, but at some point I realized that I felt worse about myself and my life. I love my friends and want them to have fun, but seeing them on vacation when I'm sitting at home bummed me out. So I decided to try a gratitude journal. At first, it felt kind of silly to journal small things, like enjoying a chocolate chip cookie. But then I realized a chocolate chip cookie is a pretty amazing thing. The journal helped me focus on appreciating what I have rather than on what I don't.
>
> —Ofelia **99**

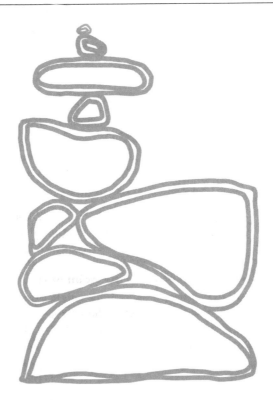

Tell Your Side of the Story

When you've actually done something wrong on social media, it doesn't help to get upset. In fact, getting upset can cause you to act before you think. This only adds to your social media stress because it complicates a situation that's already complicated. When you've done something wrong—either by mistake or on purpose—tell your side of the story but tell it in a way that shows you and your actions in the best light. The way you explain your side of the story can affect how people react and what they do. Try for stories with the following ingredients:

- **Tell the truth.** Telling your side of the story doesn't mean you lie or even minimize your part in the problem. It means you present the truth in a way that reflects your best self.

- **Say you're sorry.** Remember, an apology calms the other person. Also, if you did something wrong, a sincere apology can repair the relationship.

- **Don't talk too much.** If you stray too far from the facts, people get confused and frustrated, or might think that you're not telling the truth. Stick to the facts and describe what happened briefly and calmly.

- **Don't blame the other person.** Nothing complicates your side of the story more than blaming the other person for what happened. If the person caught you with your hand in the cookie jar, admit it.

- **Listen actively.** If you're not communicating clearly, the other person might think that you're being defensive or arguing. Remember to clarify and repeat back what you heard to signal that you're understanding what the other person is communicating.

- **Use I-statements to describe your point of view.** You-statements put people on the defensive. Use I-statements to explain your take on things, including how you felt. Rather than, "You never mention me in your posts," try, "I feel upset when you mention our friends but you don't mention me in your posts."

Try It Here Too: Telling your side of the story works for any mistake, accident, or when you're caught with your hand in the cookie jar. The stories have the same ingredients, whether it's about getting busted by your parents for coming home too late, or about telling a friend that you're sick and can't attend her party on Saturday and then seeing her at the mall that afternoon.

> **"** I got so busted! Yesterday, I posted a joke about Jesse's taste in shoes. We joke around with each other, but turns out joking on social media is tricky. Jesse didn't like it. He said he didn't mind joking with each other but he didn't like sharing the joke with everyone on our feeds. Jesse was really upset and I get why now. I knew there wasn't any point in lying and trying to say it wasn't about him. He knows my sense of humor and it was right there. So, I decided to start with an apology. It was hard, because I was already feeling defensive, but it helped. Jesse settled down so that I could explain, and I did. I told him that I wasn't thinking. It never occurred to me that I was including other people in the joke on Jesse, which is really dumb of me when you think about it. I couldn't believe it worked, but it did. Not only did Jesse calm down, but he told me that he understood that it was a mistake and that we were still cool. That helped me feel a lot better.
>
> —Deion **"**

HANDLE CYBERBULLYING

Cyberbullying involves other people making harassing or threatening comments online or spreading rumors about you or your friends and family. Most teens have been cyberbullied at one point in time, and many are cyberbullied on an ongoing basis. Cyberbullying is particularly common on platforms where messages immediately disappear, wiping out the evidence within seconds. Cyberbullying takes many forms, from a hurtful text to physical threats against you or someone you know.

EXAMPLES OF CYBERBULLYING

Posting mean or hurtful comments about someone based on their race, religion, ethnicity, or sexual orientation.

Posting mean or hurtful photos or videos of someone.

Pretending to be someone else to post false information about someone.

Creating blogs or websites that have stories, cartoons, pictures, or jokes ridiculing someone.

Hacking into someone's gaming or social networking profile.

Verbally abusing other players in multiplayer online games, internet-connected console games, and virtual worlds.

Posting rumors or comments about someone that are embarrassing, mean, or hurtful.

Stealing someone's password and impersonating them online.

Breaking into an email account and sending hurtful materials to someone under an assumed identity.

Threatening someone online, or telling them to kill themselves.

Creating fake Facebook or Twitter accounts that ridicule someone.

Posting private or embarrassing photos of someone online or sending them to other people.

Sending mean or hurtful messages to someone.

Messaging someone and tricking them into revealing personal information and then forwarding that information to others.

Spreading gossip, secrets, or rumors about someone that will damage their reputation.

Starting a website or account that rates someone's appearance or popularity.

Dealing with cyberbullying is stressful and can have serious, even life-threatening, consequences for you and your friends. Learning to protect yourself and your friends from cyberbullying is an important media and technology stress management skill:

- **Ignore.** If you or a friend appear in a negative post, don't respond. Cyberbullies want attention. Fighting back just gives them more online time for more attacks.

- **Record.** If you or a friend are cyberbullied, record and save the evidence. Take screenshots of any cyberbullying messages you receive on all your social media accounts. It's easier to identify the bully if they bully you on multiple accounts.

- **Report.** If you or a friend are cyberbullied, report the bullying to your parents or to another trusted adult immediately. Teachers, school administrators, advisors, and guidance counselors understand cyberbullying and can help you deal with it. If you're bullied via a website, report the bully to the website administrator, who may kick them off the site. In many cases, you can report cyberbullying to the safety center of the social media platform. Safety center staff may be able to uncover an anonymous bully and perhaps take down offensive posts.

- **Reach Out.** If you or a friend are cyberbullied, talk to other friends or a counselor to help you cope with the hurtful comments. There's no reason to suffer alone.

- **Cut Off.** If you're cyberbullied, stop all communication with the bully. For example, block their phone number so that you no longer receive their calls or texts. Block them from the social media platforms you use. If it's not possible to block a cyberbully, screen their calls and delete their messages without opening them.

"   I freaked out when I saw the comment on my Instagram. It was from a guy I met at a party. He asked me out and I nicely told him I wasn't interested. Then he started to comment mean things on all my posts! I wanted to call him out, but I decided to ignore him. I took screen shots as evidence and showed them to my friends. They convinced me to show them to Ms. Abramson, the librarian. She's tech-savvy and knew what to do. She tracked the guy down and reported him. The bullying stopped. I decided that I was going to limit my social media connections to only people I knew really well. A thousand followers isn't worth the hassle and the stress!

—Ofelia   **"**

Deal with Boredom Off-Device

Constant connection to devices leaves little time for the natural flow of creative thoughts and wonderment. As soon as you feel bored, you reach for your device or go to a screen. When you set aside time to daydream, to imagine, to ride the flow of your creative mind, you push away boredom and stress, too. Next time you're bored, let your mind disconnect from a device, and reconnect with your creative side:

- **Make a top 10 list.** This is a really good one because it can quickly sweep you away into a fun, creative flow. List your Top 10 movies, or your Top 10 books. List your Top 10 sports teams, or Top 10 favorite vacations. List your Top 10 songs or Top 10 meals or Top 10 colors, cookies, or words. You could even write a Top 10 list about things that bore you.

- **Make a bucket list.** Making a bucket list is easy and fun. You can do this with friends or while waiting for the bus. You might include in the bucket list the #1 of each Top 10 list. Whatever interests you, add to your bucket list. A cool thing about bucket lists is they get you thinking about adventures, doing fun things off-line, and planning for them.

- **Imagine life on a deserted island.** Imagine that you're lost and stranded on a deserted island for life. What object would you bring and why? If the object was food, would it be potatoes or chocolate chip cookies? What would life be like if all you had to eat was chocolate chip cookies? This is a fun game to play with friends, too. Encourage your friends to put away their devices on the carpool ride home, or over lunch, or while waiting for the movie to start.

- **Go for a walk.** This one is good because it stimulates both your brain and your body. There's something about exercise that gets the creative juices flowing. On the walk, look for something you've never noticed before. Connect with your five senses. What do you see, smell, and hear? How does the path feel beneath your feet? What does the air taste like, or the gum you're chewing?

- **Try something new.** Novelty is a great way to turn on your creative mind. Walk home a different way. Build a blanket fort to study under, rather than on your bed. Try a black bean rather than a pinto bean burrito. Wear a different color combination when you dress in the morning, or use different color pens to write. Break those routines, mix things up, and look for opportunities to think and act in new ways.

- **Make it into an adventure.** Through adventure, we harness creativity to live full and fun lives. Next time you eat at your favorite restaurant, select something adventurous from the menu, or nibble something strange off your friend's plate. Drive a different way to school. Find a fun destination that's close to home that you've never visited. Adventures are about getting out of your comfort zone.

- **Make it into a game.** Rather than reaching for your phone when you have to fold laundry or vacuum your room, turn the activity into a game. Dance while you vacuum. Eat a bowl of ice cream with a fork. Put away your clothes with your eyes closed. Skip to the garbage can on trash day.

Next time you reach for your device, check in with yourself. Do you feel bored, or do you feel antsy, anxious, or stressed? As you pay attention, you'll notice patterns in when, where, and why you reach for your device. Learning to deal with boredom without using your devices takes time and practice. The first step in dealing with boredom off-device is to develop a plan that includes what you'll do in certain situations rather than reaching for your device. Look at Deion's *Deal with Boredom Off-Device Exercise* to see how he did it.

DEION'S DEAL WITH BOREDOM OFF-DEVICE EXERCISE

Situation	On-Device Activity	Off-Device Activity	What I Learned
In bed in morning.	Check social media feeds, text friends.	Slow deep breathing for 5 minutes, with positive visualization.	I feel stressed before school. Breathing helps more than texting my friends, which sometimes stresses me more.

Situation	On-Device Activity	Off-Device Activity	What I Learned
Eating breakfast.	Read news, text friends.	Eat mindfully.	Pancakes tasted great.
On bus to school.	Play games, text friends.	Talk to friends, or study for quiz.	Talking to friends is more fun than texting friends who aren't there.
Before first class.	Check social media feeds, text friends.	Talk to friends.	When I talked to my friends, they stopped texting.
Lunch at school.	Check social media feeds, play games.	Talk to friends.	More fun than playing games.
On bus home.	Text friends, play games.	Talk to friends, or get started on homework.	Getting started on homework helps.
Before homework.	Watch YouTube, text friends.	Slow deep breathing for 5 minutes, organize homework.	Homework stresses me out, breathing relaxes me.
During homework breaks.	Watch YouTube, text friends.	Meditate for 5 minutes.	I felt calmer and more productive.
Dinner with family.	Text friends.	Talk and joke with my family.	My family is a riot.
After homework.	Binge-watch television shows.	Play cards with sister and talk.	My sister is fun to talk to.
Before bed.	Text friends, check social media feeds.	Read a book, drink cup of tea.	Slept better and felt more relaxed.

> **“** I never realized how often I reach for my phone when I'm bored. It's automatic. I decided that for two weeks I would do something else when I was bored, to see what that was like. I decided to try to do two off-device activities for every on-device activity. I still get bored—who doesn't—but I'm dealing with it better, I think. Not only that, taking a break showed me that a lot of my on-device activities, like checking my social media feeds, made me feel stressed and sometimes downright unhappy. That's a big price to pay just to feel less bored.
> —Deion **”**

-🔅-STRESS HACK: Social media use can bring some good stuff, but some bad stuff too. If you're feeling fine about your social media habits, no problem. But, if you're feeling stressed, unhappy, and disconnected, it might make sense to take a social media detox. First, decide the length of the detox you'll take. It can be as brief as a week or as long as a year. Yes, some people swear off social media for a year, and some people swear off it forever! Once you've decided the length of the detox, deactivate your social media accounts and delete the apps from your phone. If you're worried that you won't maintain your social media detox, try apps like Freedom and Self Control to limit your access to Instagram and Facebook on your phone and computer.

🌰 In a Nutshell

Media and technology use is a growing source of stress for people, and this kind of stress isn't going away. Teens in particular have to manage the stress of media overload and media relationships, and fit it in to schedules that are already jammed with classes, homework, and fun with friends. Learning skills to manage media and technology stress are vital to life in an ever-expanding online world.

CHAPTER 8

Health and Hormone Stress

Healthy eating, reasonable exercise, and adequate sleep make up the foundation on which you build any plan to manage stress. Yet stressed teens often forget the foundation when they're stressed, which only adds to their stress, because it takes a healthy mind and body to manage stress in the first place. It's a vicious cycle! Learning skills to take care of your health, as well as skills to manage the stress that comes with the significant fluctuations in hormone levels for most teens, will build a mind and body that are more resilient, capable, and calm. In this chapter, you'll learn the following skills to deal with health and hormone stress:

- Build a Consistent Sleep Schedule
- Build a Sleep Wind-Down Routine
- Deal with Unfinished Business
- Savor to Sleep Better
- Tell Your Body to Relax
- Build an Out-of-Bed-in-the-Morning Plan
- Build a Stay-Alert Plan
- Try Yoga Instead of Yawns
- Exercise Your Way to a Calmer Self
- Eat Your Way to a Calmer Self

Build a Consistent Sleep Schedule

Your body ticks according to many internal biological clocks, and your brain operates all of them. These biological clocks control many things: mood, body temperature, hunger, release of hormones. You have a biological clock that controls sleep, too. This biological sleep clock controls sleepiness, your optimal sleep window, and alertness. The alertness function of your sleep clock rises and falls reliably over a 24-hour period. Most teens are night owls. They feel the least alert in the morning hours, with increasing alertness in the afternoon until they feel the most alert, awake, and ready to go in the evening. Then alertness starts to fall again very late in the evening or early morning hours. Although your sleep clock is ticking like a night owl now, the clock may shift more to a morning lark (most alert in the morning hours and least alert early in the evening) as you grow older. Most adults are a mix of both sleep types: not fully a morning lark and not fully a night owl. Regardless of your sleep type, your sleep clock is a powerful internal force that influences the quality of your sleep. The best way to harness that power is to send your clock consistent signals that keep it ticking on a regular schedule:

- **Maintain consistent sleep goalposts.** Your lights-out time and get-out-of-bed time are the goalposts that help to keep your basic sleep-wake cycle normal. With consistent sleep goalposts your brain can better determine when it's time to light up for activity and when it's time to dim for sleep. Of course, you want to have a life. At times you'll want to stay out late with friends or participate in early morning extracurricular activities. But try to maintain a regular bedtime and rise time with just occasional changes. This will make a big difference in how you sleep at night and how you feel during the day.

- **Avoid sleeping in on weekends.** If you're like most teens, you don't get enough sleep from Monday through Friday. You likely stay up late in the evening to finish schoolwork, take part in extracurricular activities, and spend time with friends and family. After a few days of this you can build up a significant sleep deficit, which means that you often struggle to wake up on time for school and to stay awake during classes. So it's understandable that you want to catch up and sleep until noon or even later on Saturday and Sunday. Although you may feel better during the weekend when you sleep in, you'll likely pay a price when Monday morning rolls around again. That's because sleeping in on weekends is like jet lag without traveling—there's a mismatch between your internal body clock and the environment. This can cause you to feel tired and moody, and can make it difficult for you to think and concentrate until your body clock adjusts to the new time. So, when you sleep in until 11:00 am on Saturday and Sunday, you'll likely have more difficulty falling asleep at your bedtime on Sunday night. And, when the alarm sounds at 6:00 am on Monday, your body clock isn't ready to wake up. That's a five-hour difference in wake time, and it will feel like it. So, try not to sleep past your usual out-of-bed time by more than one or two hours.

- **Maintain consistent activities.** Your sleep clock is sensitive to activities too. Try to eat your meals on a regular schedule. If you exercise regularly, try to do that at around the same time every day, too. If you walk the family dog, try to do it around the same time. And even think about the time you spend with family and friends. Your sleep clock is sensitive to social activities, too. Fun and consistent activities lift your mood, and when you feel better you'll sleep better.

- **Follow the light.** Light signals your brain to light up. Try to get as much sunlight as you can after waking. Light not only sweeps away those sleepy cobwebs, but it sets your sleep clock for the day. When you wake up, immediately open your bedroom blinds or curtains and stretch and move gently in the sunlight. Turn on all the lights in your bedroom. Don't wear hoodies or sunglasses in the morning, and do sit in the sunlight when you have breakfast, if you can.

-☼- *STRESS HACK:* Don't forget the little things when it comes to sleep. Keep your bedroom quiet, dark, and cool. Darkness and coolness send important signals to your brain to slow down and shift toward sleep. Also, if you use a nightlight, try to place it so that you can't see it from bed, and don't look at any light when you get up in the night for a sip of water. Warm hands are a sign of a relaxed body, so do what you can to relax your body prior to bedtime. Slip on some socks and tuck your hands under the blankets. Don't eat a big meal or snack before bedtime. Your body isn't meant to digest meals when you sleep. If you're hungry, try a small, healthy snack. If you can, take a hot bath before bed. A hot soak increases your body temperature slightly. Then, when you hop out, you'll cool down quickly, which mimics the natural drop in body temperature caused by the brain as it readies the body for sleep.

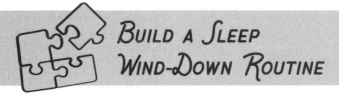

Build a Sleep Wind-Down Routine

When you're stressed, you likely have a busy mind, and a busy mind can make it difficult to settle down and sleep at bedtime. A sleep wind-down routine is a powerful way to signal your mind that it's time to relax, to unwind, and to move toward sleep. However, as important as a wind-down routine is, don't wind-down in your bed, particularly when it takes you a long time to fall asleep. You want to reserve your bed for sleep, and sleep only. In fact, when you study in bed, or watch a show in bed, or read your social media feeds in bed, you train your brain to be alert and awake in bed. Wind down outside of your bed and then get into bed when you're sleepy. Remember, though, sleepy isn't the same as tired. Sleepy means that your mind and body are hungry for sleep. That's when you have to re-read the same page over and over, and feel your eyelids closing or your head dropping forward or snapping back. These are signs that it's time to go to bed.

The best sleep wind-down routine is one that's simple and personal. Try to include strategies in your wind-down routine that use all your senses (sight, sound, taste, smell, touch) to signal your brain that it's time to slow down for sleep. Build sleep wind-down routines that include things that you'll use *only* to wind down for sleep. For example, drink the same herbal tea from the same mug, or listen to the same music, or burn the same scented candle. Below are several strategies that you could include in your wind-down routine:

- Take a warm bath or shower.
- Listen to a guided relaxation recording.
- Listen to calming music that you play.
- Stretch gently for 10 minutes.
- Meditate for 10 minutes.
- Breathe slowly and deeply for 10 minutes.
- Drink, smell, and hold a cup of herbal tea.
- Massage your face and hands with a scented lotion.
- Curl up in your warm bed and savor the good things that happened that day.

- Say a mantra to yourself for five minutes (for example, "silver moon, cobalt night, easy sleep").

- Write in your journal the good things about the day for 10 minutes.

Now that you've identified several wind-down strategies that you might want to include in your personalized wind-down routine, follow these steps to build your own sleep wind-down routine:

1. On a blank sheet of paper, list each step in your wind-down routine. Remember to include wind-down strategies that you'll use only as part of this routine.

2. On the back page of your sleep wind-down routine or on a calendar, each day write the number that corresponds to how well the wind-down routine helped prepare your mind and body for sleep. Use a 0 to 10 scale (where 10 is a bull's eye, 5 is close but not great, and 0 is not helpful at all).

You may want to try several different wind-down routines until you find one that really and truly works best for you. Try the wind-down routine for at least a week. To get an idea of how to do this, look at Ofelia's.

OFELIA'S SLEEP WIND-DOWN ROUTINE EXERCISE

1. Place the soft plush wind-down pillow on my bed. Settle into the pillow and pull up the covers so that I'm warm and cozy.

2. Turn off all the lights except for the small bedside table lamp.

3. Write in my gratitude journal for 10 minutes. Describe at least three things that happened during the day that I'm grateful for.

4. Sip a cup of warm chamomile tea from my special wind-down mug. Inhale the warm fragrance of the chamomile tea steeping in the mug.

5. Listen to my wind-down music playlist that has the same relaxing songs I like.

6. As I listen to the music, massage my hands with the special wind-down lotion.

-💡- *STRESS HACK:* Most teens don't get enough sleep during the week because they're up late studying and then up very early for school. That doesn't leave much opportunity to sleep, plain and simple. To create more time to sleep, move some of your morning routine (for example, showering, making your lunch, organizing your backpack, selecting your clothes) to the night before. Also, move that important wind-down routine as early as you can in order to get to bed early enough for as much sleep as possible.

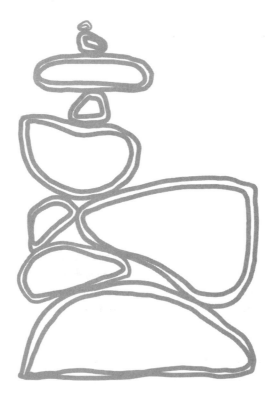

DEAL WITH UNFINISHED BUSINESS

Unfinished business is the concerns or problems that arose during the day—an argument with a friend, a dropped pass in the game, a bad grade on the quiz, the tear in your jeans—that you didn't have time to think through or solve because you were just too busy doing what you needed to do to get through the day. That's why unfinished business hits you at bedtime. Bedtime is the first time that life has slowed down enough that your brain has time to think through and solve the unfinished business of the day. Now, you're lying awake in bed thinking through an endless string of solutions, one after another. If this sounds like you, follow these steps to deal with unfinished business:

1. Several hours before bed, when you're rested and clear-headed, sit down with a blank sheet of paper. Draw a line down the middle of the paper and at the top of the left column write *Concerns* and at the top of the right column write *Solutions*.

2. In the *Concerns* column, list all the concerns that might keep you awake at bedtime. For example, in the *Concerns* column you might write, "I bombed the history exam," or "I blew up at Jesse at lunch."

3. For each concern, write in the *Solutions* column the first step you'll take to solve the problem tomorrow. This may not be the final solution to the problem, because you solve most problems in steps anyway, so just write the first step. It's okay to guess.

4. If you know how to solve the problem completely, write that solution (for example, "I'll speak to Mr. Samuel about whether I can get some extra credit to bring up my history grade") in the *Solution* column. If you decide that the concern is not really a big problem and that you'll just deal with it when the time comes, then write that (for example, "I'll wait to see my progress report next week before I speak to Mr. Samuel"). If you decide you just don't know what to do about the problem, and that you'll ask someone to help you, write that (for example, "I'll ask Janie if she did anything to bring up her grade in Mr. Samuel's class."). Last, if you decide that it's a problem but there isn't a good solution to it at all, which means that you'll just have

to live with it, write that down. Add a note to remind yourself that sometime soon you or someone you know will give you a clue that will lead to a solution (for example, "There isn't any solution to this problem. I bet I'll learn something tomorrow or the next day that could solve the problem, but in the meantime, I'll just live with it").

5.   Fold the worksheet in half and on the blank side of the paper write:
   •   I've dealt with my concerns already in the best way I know how, when I was rested and at my problem-solving best. Therefore, I'm not likely to come up with a better first step than the one I came up with earlier.
   •   I'll work on the concerns tomorrow and I'll start with the first step. There's nothing I can do right now when I'm in bed, foggy headed and tired. In fact, working more on the problem in my head will only keep me awake. Then, I'll be tired tomorrow, which will only make it harder for me to solve the concerns.

6.   Set the folded piece of paper on the nightstand next to your bed. Tell yourself to forget about it until bedtime. At bedtime, if you catch yourself slipping into unfinished business, remind yourself of what you wrote on the other side of the paper.

Check out Asif's *Deal with Unfinished Business Exercise* to see how to do this.

ASIF'S DEAL WITH UNFINISHED BUSINESS EXERCISE

Concern	Solution
I bombed the history exam.	I'll talk to Mr. Samuel about whether I can get some extra credit to bring up my history grade.
I blew up at Jesse at lunch.	I'll find him tomorrow morning and apologize.
The screen on my phone is cracked.	I'll ask Mom if I can borrow some money to repair it and pay her back when I get my allowance.

| Coach wants to talk to me after practice tomorrow. | There isn't any solution to this concern so I'll just let it go. Tomorrow coach will tell me and I'll handle the problem then, if there is a problem. |
| My history book isn't in my backpack. | It's either in my locker or in the history classroom. I'll check both before my first class. |

I've dealt with my concerns already in the best way I know how, when I was rested and at my problem-solving best. Therefore, I'm not likely to come up with a better first step than the one I came up with earlier.

I'll work on the concerns tomorrow and I'll start with the first step. There's nothing I can do right now anyway when I'm in bed, foggy headed and tired. In fact, working more on the problem will only keep me awake and then I'll be tired tomorrow, which will only make it harder for me to solve the concerns.

66 I always lie in bed thinking about the things I have to do the next day. It's usually small stuff, like checking my locker for my math book or talking to one of my teachers about an assignment. Before, I would always try not to think about it, but my mind kept going round and round. It was exhausting and a great way to stay awake when I want to sleep. The first time I tried the Deal With Unfinished Business skill I thought there was no way it would work, but it did. It was actually kind of a relief to know

I had already thought about those things and put them aside. Now I know how to deal with the unfinished business in my head so that I can sleep! —Asif

99

STRESS HACK: As one stressful day leads to another, it may feel like you're walking through a fog of stress and worry. Try this simple trick to climb out of a stressful moment in order to see things as they really are. Sit in a comfortable chair and close your eyes. Now, imagine your stress is like a dense, heavy fog that's swirling around you. Take several deep breaths as you imagine standing and walking up a hill. With each step, softly say to yourself, *relax and refresh,* as you walk up the hill and the fog thins. Continue to imagine walking up the hill as the fog becomes thinner and thinner until you reach the top of the hill. Now, take a moment and look around. Below you is the fog of stress, churning and swirling. Before you are mountain tops, a bright blue sky, and a beautiful valley spreading out before you as far as you can see. Take several deep breaths as you softly say to yourself, *relax and refresh.* Finish by resting several minutes above the hustle and bustle of stress at your feet.

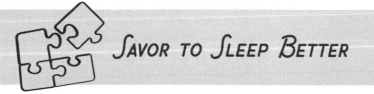

Savor to Sleep Better

Savoring is a great way to decrease stress while you're waiting for sleep to come. Not only does savoring give you something to think about, but it also creates pleasant feelings to counter the frustration you sometimes feel when sleep isn't coming as quickly as you would like. Savoring means enjoying a pleasant taste or smell, such as savoring the taste and smell of a warm chocolate chip cookie. You can savor memories too, particularly memories of feeling happy or comfortable. For example, feeling excited and happy the time you won a soccer game, or feeling warm and safe wrapped in your grandmother's arms. Savoring a memory works best when you try to remember everything about it—where you were and when it happened, who you were with, and what you were feeling and thinking. To create a memory to savor at bedtime, follow these steps:

1. List three good times you had recently (favorite activities, favorite places you've visited, good times you've shared with friends or family, successes in your life, whatever).

2. Pick one of the good times and picture it in your mind. Write the elements of the good time into a story. Who was there? What were you doing? How were you feeling? What were you thinking?

3. Close your eyes and savor the good time story by replaying it in your mind several times.

4. Rate the intensity of the image and the intensity of the good feelings you feel (low, medium, high).

5. Practice replaying the good time story in your mind until the intensity of the image and the good feelings are high. Feel free to add other elements to the story in order to create intense good feelings.

6. Now practice savoring the good time story while you wait for sleep to come at bedtime, or for it to come back if you awaken in the middle of the night. If you like, create a list of good feeling stories and place the list nearby when your good time story gets a bit stale and you want to savor another one.

✍ TRY IT HERE TOO: In addition to savor to sleep better, you can savor to interrupt your mind's tendency to worry at bedtime. To savor to interrupt worry, follow these steps:

1. *Worry:* Worry for two minutes. Think of a situation that you're worrying about. It might be about friends, school, family, health, or anything else. Give yourself complete freedom to worry about the situation. Don't hold back. Worry intensely! But after two minutes, stop.

2. *Savor:* Savor for two minutes one of the good time stories you created earlier. Remember to think about all the pieces of the story (where you where, when it happened, who was there, and what you were feeling and thinking).

3. *Shift:* Shift between worrying for two minutes and savoring for two minutes. Continue this activity while you wait for sleep to come (or to come back).

Tell Your Body to Relax

Believe it or not, you can tell your body to relax. In this quick relaxation skill, you'll prepare your mind and body for sleep. To tell your body to relax, follow these steps:

1. Lie down in bed and close your eyes. Tell the following groups of muscles to relax, and as you do, visualize the feeling of relaxation flowing into the muscle group:
   - My forehead and scalp feel heavy, limp, loose, and relaxed.
   - My eyes and nose feel heavy, limp, loose, and relaxed.
   - My face and jaws feel heavy, limp, loose, and relaxed.
   - My neck, shoulders, and back feel heavy, limp, loose, and relaxed.
   - My arms and hands feel heavy, limp, loose, and relaxed.
   - My chest and stomach feel heavy, limp, loose, and relaxed.
   - My buttocks and thighs feel heavy, limp, loose, and relaxed.
   - My calves, ankles, and toes feel heavy, limp, loose, and relaxed.
   - My entire body feels heavy, limp, and relaxed.

2. Repeat this sequence two or three times. Try to practice twice a day for 8–10 minutes. In a couple of weeks you'll feel yourself slipping into relaxation when you close your eyes and wait for sleep to come.

BUILD AN OUT-OF-BED-IN-THE-MORNING PLAN

When you don't' sleep well or sleep enough, it's tough to wake up and get out of bed in the morning. You linger in bed as you repeatedly push the snooze button, hoping that you'll sleep, at least for a few minutes more — but sleep doesn't come. At least not real sleep. Snooze button sleep is restless, fitful, and shallow. It's not good quality sleep. In fact, it's not really sleep at all. If you want to sleep better the next night, get up and get going in the morning rather than lingering in bed trying to get more sleep. An out-of-bed-in-the-morning plan will help.

No two out-of-the-bed-in-the-morning plans are the same. Some people favor a bitter cold shower to get them going. Others like to sing and dance to their favorite tunes and ease more slowly into the day. But the best out-of-the-bed-in-the-morning strategies always include three things: light, movement, and a bit of fun.

Look at the list of wake-up strategies. Perhaps you can't imagine using a particular strategy (a cold shower in the morning), or you would use a particular strategy but your family wouldn't be cool with it (crowing like a rooster). Which strategies do you use or would you consider using? Which strategies are off the table for you?

EXAMPLES OF WAKE-UP STRATEGIES

Take an ice cold shower.	Crow like a rooster or Peter Pan.
Dance to your favorite tune for two minutes.	Jog in place for two minutes.
Sing at the top of your lungs for two minutes.	Play air guitar to your favorite song.
Take five deep slow breaths and flap your arms like an eagle.	Open curtains (and eyes) and stand in the sun for two minutes.
Listen to a high-energy song for two minutes.	Drink a cup of tea or coffee.
Yawn five times and make a loud noise when inhaling.	Kick off the covers and make a snow angel in the bed sheets.

Try building a personalized Out-of-Bed-in-the-Morning Plan and see how it works. On a blank piece of paper, list the steps of your plan. Try the plan for a week. Feel free to change the plan until it works for you. You may want to try several different strategies until you have a plan that really and truly works for you. Look at Alesandro's *Out-of-Bed-in-the-Morning Plan* to see how to do this.

ALESANDRO'S OUT-OF-BED-IN-THE-MORNING PLAN

1. Turn on bedside light, sit up, put in earbuds.
2. Play the theme from Rocky.
3. Stand up, open curtains, and do jumping jacks until the end of the song.
4. Shadow-box for a minute to theme from Rocky, again.
5. Take hot shower but finish with five seconds of cold water.
6. Dress while I listen to another high-energy song.
7. Have a cup of tea and breakfast.

STRESS HACK: Bend and breathe is another quick breathing technique. It's a great way to clear your head, relax your body, and boost your energy. Try it when you first get out of bed in the morning:

1. Stand and slowly bend forward from the waist with your knees slightly bent. Let your arms dangle close to the floor.

2. Inhale slowly and deeply as you slowly roll your body up to a standing position, lifting your head last.

3. Hold your breath for three seconds in this standing position.

4. Exhale slowly as you return to the original position, bending forward from the waist.

Build a Stay-Alert Plan

Sleep fatigue means that you're not getting all the sleep that your mind and body require. Your body feels heavy and slow. You have trouble concentrating or thinking clearly. You feel more irritable than usual. To fight sleep fatigue and give your mind a natural boost too, try the following:

- **Move.** Move your body to fight sleep fatigue. It takes energy to make energy and even a little physical activity can push away fatigue. Movement and activity generate energy and turn on your brain. Also, boredom intensifies feelings of fatigue. So stand up, stretch, and move around your bedroom a little to counter moments of boredom or mental fatigue when you're studying. Avoid vigorous exercise too close to your lights-out time, though; you don't want to light up your brain when you want it to downshift and prepare to sleep.

- **Light.** Bathing in natural sunlight is a great way to push away sleep fatigue. Indoor light is the next best thing. When you're feeling fatigued, open the curtains or turn on the lights. During the day, sit in the sunlight to study. At night, darken your room one or two hours before bedtime, and use as little light as possible to signal your brain to down shift and prepare to sleep.

- **Hydrate.** Drink water during the day, particularly if you play sports or it's a hot day. You might feel tired because you're dehydrated. Many teens drink caffeinated or sugary beverages throughout the day to fight tiredness, but pay the price at night when they're ready to sleep but can't because of these substances. Not only that, caffeinated beverages can dehydrate you, which can then worsen the tiredness you feel. Limit yourself to one caffeinated drink in the morning and avoid sugary drinks as much as possible.

- **Eat.** Eat a healthy meal three times a day. When you skip meals or eat junk foods with a lot of carbohydrates or sugar, you create sudden shifts in your blood sugar levels. These shifts can cause you to feel tired, weak, and make it difficult for you to concentrate. Plus, regular meals help your sleep clock tick consistently.

- **Change.** Change up activities to stay alert. If you're studying for a math exam, shift to outlining the English essay due next week. Math and English work different parts of your brain, so shifting from one task to another gives that part of your brain a little break. Also, when you're tired, break larger projects into smaller tasks. Trying to stay focused for a long time is exhausting, and particularly exhausting when you're already tired. Work at the smaller tasks in short, scheduled bursts. Use a timer and work for 20 minutes and then take a two-minute break.

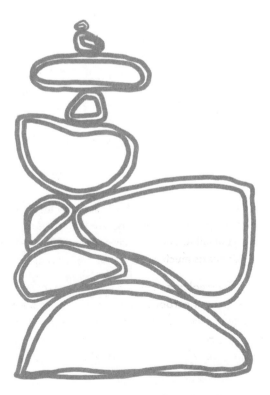

Try Yoga Instead of Yawns

Yoga can increase your flexibility and fitness, and decrease your stress. Yoga is also a great way to energize your mind and body when you're feeling tired or fatigued during the day. In fact, certain yoga poses are particularly energizing. Here are three quick energizing yoga poses:

Mountain pose: This basic pose is very energizing because you feel the energy of the universe in your body. To begin the Mountain pose, stand with the bases of your big toes together and your heels slightly apart. Rock onto your heels so that you can lift your toes and the balls of your feet. Fully spread and fan out your toes as you elevate them, and then lay your toes comfortably spaced back on the floor. Make sure your weight is well-balanced between your two feet. Tighten your quads to lift your kneecaps, and allow your inner thighs to rotate slightly inward. Contract your pelvic floor muscles and abdomen so that your body is nice and tall. Take a deep breath, broadening your collarbones and drawing your shoulder blades back. Relax your face and imagine the crown of your head reaching high up to the sky as you elongate your spine.

Chair pose: This pose can help you feel strong, powerful, and energized because you're using some of the biggest muscles in your body: primarily your thigh and butt muscles. Also, with your arms extended overhead, you'll stretch your back, shoulders, and chest, opening your heart and lungs and encouraging blood flow and oxygen throughout your body. To begin the chair pose, start in Mountain pose. Then exhale as you lower your body down into a squat, while you shift your hips back as if sitting in a chair. Inhale as you lift your arms over your head. Sink lower into the squat, as you reach up higher with your arms. Hold for four to five breaths and then press through your heels to stand into mountain pose and return your arms to your sides.

Standing Forward Bend pose: This pose has many physical and mental benefits that energize the body, clear the mind, and reset your system. To begin the standing forward bend pose, start in Mountain pose with your knees slightly bent and your feet hip-width apart. Bend at your hips so that your upper body hangs down over your legs and your arms and hands fall comfortably toward your legs and ankles. Hang in this position while taking deep breaths, gently swaying back and forth from one side to the other, and alternate between nodding your head "yes" and shaking your head "no." To return to standing, draw your navel toward your spine, and slowly roll up one vertebra at a time.

TRY IT HERE TOO: Yoga is a great way to relieve period cramps, too. Although your body may feel like it's telling you to stay in bed and under the covers all day, it's gentle movement, not bed rest, that will help the most. The Head-to-Knee pose eases cramp pain and boosts your energy. Sit with your legs extended. Bend your right knee and position your right foot on the inside of your left upper thigh. Inhale and lift your arms overhead. Then, exhale and lean forward over your left leg, and rest your forehead on your thigh (or on a pillow)—if you can't get all the way down, don't worry! Just bend as far as you can comfortably. Hold this pose for 30 seconds, then inhale to sit up. Switch sides and repeat.

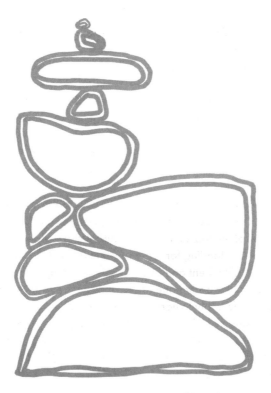

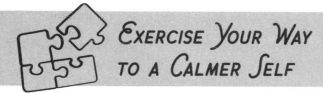

EXERCISE YOUR WAY TO A CALMER SELF

Exercise is a powerful way to reduce stress, and you'll notice the benefits for hours and days afterward, not just while you exercise. When we exercise, magical things happen. We release chemicals in our brains and bodies that neutralize stress chemicals and stimulate the release of "happiness chemicals" called endorphins. These "happiness chemicals" are a powerful antidote to stress. Plus, there are other benefits to regular exercise:

- **Exercise builds self-confidence and self-esteem.** When you exercise regularly, you'll grow stronger mentally and physically and therefore more confident that you can handle life's challenges. And, as you grow stronger and more coordinated, you'll feel better about yourself, and this will increase your self-esteem and social confidence.

- **Exercise sharpens memory and thinking.** The same "happiness chemicals" that reduce your stress also help you concentrate and feel mentally sharp. Exercise also stimulates the growth of new brain cells that can help you learn and thrive.

- **Exercise improves sleep.** Even short bursts of exercise in the morning or afternoon can help regulate your sleep patterns. Exercise improves the quality of your sleep because you'll sleep more deeply. If you prefer to exercise at night, relaxing exercises such as yoga or gentle stretching can help promote sleep.

- **Exercise increases energy.** Although you expend energy when you exercise, over time, you increase your body's energy reserves. More energy gives you more get-up-and-go, which counters the fatigue you feel when you're stressed and run-down. Also, with more energy you'll get more things off your to-do list, which will lessen your stress and increase your effectiveness.

- **Exercise increases resilience.** Exercise improves your ability to bounce back from the physical and emotional challenges you face. As you build an exercise habit, you'll notice that the small tasks that once overwhelmed you now seem more reasonable and doable.

To begin your exercise program, start by creating a plan. An effective exercise plan includes the exercise you'll do, the amount you'll do, and when you'll do it:

Decide on the Type of Exercise

Remember, the best exercise is the one you'll do regularly, so build a list of exercises that you can do every day, such as dancing, running, or walking. You can also include exercises that are fun when you can do them, such as golf or snowboarding, just remember that these types of exercise require some planning and they're generally not the kind of thing you can do several days each week, week after week:

TYPES OF REGULAR EXERCISE			
Basketball	Climbing steps	Power walking	Swimming
Biking	Dancing	Rowing machine	Walking
Calisthenics	Exercise bike	Running	Weight lifting
Circuit training	Jumping rope	Shadow boxing	Yoga

Decide How Often and When

Remember to set a realistic goal that starts where you are. If you haven't exercised in a long time, set a goal of exercising once or twice each week. Again, be realistic. If you're not a morning person, consider exercising a little later in the day, but not late in the evening. Late exercise might keep you awake when you want to sleep.

Decide How Much Time You'll Exercise

Remember to start small, perhaps fifteen minutes at first, and then increase the amount of time you exercise over the next few months. To make exercise more fun, consider asking a friend to be your exercise buddy.

-⚙- *STRESS HACK:* Exercise is exercise, and it helps to broaden the definition of exercise to increase the likelihood that you'll get your daily dose. For example, walking your dog is exercise. Volunteer more often to walk Fido before and after school. Just 20 minutes of walking your dog is enough. Explore your town or neighborhood. Just walk out your front door. It's fun to discover hidden steps on the hillside, or an interesting house you've never seen. Then, share your discoveries at mealtimes with your family. They may want to check out the neighborhood too. Next time you and your friends have lunch, suggest a quick walk after you've eaten, or walk around the campus (if allowed) to catch up on the latest news or gossip. Or, if you attend after-school club meetings, suggest you take the meeting for a walk if the weather is good. Walking will clear your mind and increase your creative sparkle. Last, when you can, stand rather than sit, run rather than walk, and take the stairs rather than the elevator. It's all exercise!

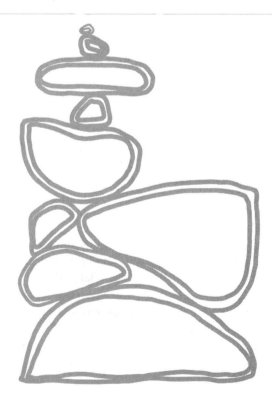

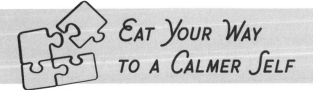

EAT YOUR WAY TO A CALMER SELF

When you're stressed, you can fall into a pattern of unhealthy eating. You might eat high calorie foods, or drink caffeinated beverages to boost your mood and energy after a day of the blahs. You might eat fast food because you're too stressed to sit down to a full healthy meal, or eat junk food because you're bored or worried about this or that. In order to eat your way to a calmer self, start with a healthy eating plan that includes the 3Ws of healthy eating:

- **What you eat.** Food fuels a body the way gas fuels a car. When you mainly fill a car's tank with low-grade fuel, you can expect that it will run poorly or even break down. Fill your tank with healthy foods first, then there will be less room for unhealthy foods. Start with colorful fruits and vegetables. Then top off the tank, if you wish, with less colorful foods, those beige and brown chips and cookies. Beware though, food companies know the trick about color. Start with foods that naturally have color rather than foods that companies add color to, such as those multi-colored chips.

- **When you eat.** When you eat can make a difference in whether an eating plan is healthy or unhealthy. Late night eating, for example, affects your biological clock. That's the clock that regulates important biological functions such as sleep, hormone secretion, blood pressure, and metabolism. Healthy eating involves eating on a reasonable schedule and avoiding late-night snacks. And try not to skip meals because you think that you're too busy or too tired or too stressed to eat. Eat small, healthy snacks if you can't eat a full healthy meal, to avoid those intense cravings that set you up to binge junk food late at night.

- **Where and how you eat.** Eating on the run or eating while doing something else isn't healthy eating because it's not mindful eating. Mindful eating is when you pay close attention to what you're eating. Mindful eating also makes you less likely to race past the "tank-is-full" warning your stomach sends to your brain when you've eaten enough. In order to eat more mindfully, don't read, text, or watch videos while you eat. If you're eating, just eat. Also, sit down when you eat. Sitting down can remind you to eat at a slower pace and pay attention to your stomach's signal that the tank is full.

🌰 In a Nutshell

A healthy body and healthy habits are the fundamentals of any plan to handle your stress. When you're not sleeping well, exercising enough, or eating healthy, everything is more difficult, including managing your stress. Learning skills to manage health and hormone stress will help you feel stronger, more confident, and better able to take on the world.

CHAPTER 9
Thriving

By now, you've learned many stress management skills. These include inside skills to calm your stressed body and thinking skills to calm your stressed mind. You've also learned outside skills, such as assertiveness, clear communication, and problem-solving, to manage the events and situations that trigger stress itself. As you've practiced these skills, you've likely noticed that life is getting easier. Less stress filled days, weeks, and months. Congratulations!

But there's more to life than just managing stress. You want to thrive. That means building a life that's fulfilling, rewarding, and meaningful, not just less stressful. In this chapter, you'll learn the following skills to thrive:

- Keep Your Balance
- Send Thank You Notes to Yourself
- Touch Hand to Heart
- Write a Letter of Recommendation for Yourself
- Meditate on Self-Acceptance
- Spend Time with Your Best Self
- Meditate on Loving Kindness
- Drink from the Cup of Optimism
- Replace Hopelessness with Hope
- Give Back

Keep Your Balance

A life filled with stress, anxiety, and worry doesn't leave much time for fun. And even if you do make time for fun, it's less fun when you rush from one fun activity to the next. If you rush around trying to fit everything into the day—fun and responsibilities—your life is likely out of balance. Now that you've learned skills to manage stress, anxiety, and worry, it's time to use those skills to get your life back in balance and keep it there. There are two steps to help you get and keep your life in balance:

Record How You Spend Your Time

Most teens spend their time between fun and proud activities and responsibilities. *Fun activities* are the fun things you do, such as going to a movie with friends, or listening to music. *Proud activities* are the things you do that make you feel good after you complete them, even though they may not always be fun while you're doing them, such as flute lessons or baseball practice. *Responsibilities* are the things you do that aren't fun but you're expected to do, like homework, chores, or a part-time job.

On a blank sheet of paper, draw four columns. In the first two columns, write your fun and proud activities and the amount of time *each week* that you spend doing these activities. In the next two columns, write the responsibilities you do and the amount of time *each week* you spend doing these responsibilities.

Develop a Keep Your Balance Plan

Next, develop a plan to get your life back in balance. No two plans are the same, because no two people are the same when it comes to their activities. The goal is to develop a weekly plan that feels balanced for you and that you're confident that you can maintain over time. For example, if your fun to responsibility ratio is 20:80, you might work toward a 30:70 or 40:60 ratio. You may want to use some of the outside skills you've learned to get your life back in balance, such as standing up for yourself, communicating calmly and clearly, solving problems, managing distractions, and scheduling time.

Look at Kanesha's *Keep Your Balance Exercise* to see how to do this. Kanesha is very busy and there isn't much fun in her week. Her fun-to-responsibility ratio is about 15:85. Kanesha made several changes to her schedule. She decided to volunteer only at the dog shelter and asked her sister to walk their dog half the week. She also decided to attend the SAT study group once rather than three times per week because she was feeling pretty good about studying on her own. She cut back a little on her field hockey drills practice at home and increased the time she played pickup games with friends for fun. She decided to help her sister a little less with math, too. Her sister was doing better, and after 30 minutes she started to get tired anyway. The first week, her fun-to-responsibility ratio was about 20:80. After a couple of weeks, Kanesha saw that she had enough time to finish her homework and cut back on that time a little and added more fun time. After about a month, her fun-to-responsibility ratio was about 30:70, which felt good for her and was something that she thought she could maintain.

-☀- *STRESS HACK:* Spending time in nature is a great way to keep your balance. Not only that, getting outdoors is good for your mental and physical health. Japanese researchers have studied the benefits of "forest bathing," which is a poetic way to say "a walk in the woods." Time outdoors can decrease your blood pressure and stress hormone levels, reduce your anxiety, and improve your mood. Just two hours a week outside can help, even if it's just lying on a blanket in the park, sitting on a bench under a beautiful tree, or making snow angels. In fact, it's more about how you spend the time outside than what you do outside. Try to savor the outside experience with all your senses rather than just taking in nature's beauty with your eyes. Sniff the air for the fragrance of honey suckle along the fence. Listen for the sound of a squirrel scurrying up a tree. Touch the grass with the tips of your toes. Taste the lemony flavor of sourgrass in the meadow. Also, search for nature pop-ups: those little surprises that make time in nature exciting and joyful. A flower in bloom, a tightly wound fern fiddlehead, the flicker of light from a puddle, or a mound of snow.

KANESHA'S KEEP YOUR BALANCE PLAN EXERCISE

My Weekly Activities and Responsibilities

Fun and Proud Activities		Responsibilities	
Activity	Time per Week	Activity	Time per Week
Play field hockey for fun	60 mins.	Homework	1,080 mins.
Dinner with grandma	120 mins.	SAT study group	180 mins.
Lunch with friends	100 mins.	Study for SAT	180 mins.
Paint	60 mins.	School	1,800 mins.
Hang with Julia	200 mins.	Tutoring	60 mins.
Watch favorite show	120 mins.	Home chores	300 mins.
		Field hockey practice	90 mins.
		Hockey drills at home	90 mins.
		Volunteer at shelter	120 mins.
		Walk dog	210 mins.
		Field hockey games	210 mins.
		Tutor sister in math	60 mins.
		Volunteer school tutor	60 mins.
Total Time per Week:	660 mins.	Total Time per Week:	4,440 mins.

My Balance Plan for the Week

Fun and Proud Activities		Responsibilities	
Activity	Time per Week	Activity	Time per Week
Play field hockey for fun	180 mins.	Homework	1,080 mins.
Dinner with grandma	120 mins.	SAT study group	60 mins.
Lunch with friends	240 mins.	Study for SAT	180 mins.
Hang with friends	120 mins.	School	1,800 mins.
Hang with Julia	360 mins	Tutoring	60 mins.
Watch favorite show	120 mins.	Home chores	300 mins.
Paint	60 mins.	Field hockey practice	90 mins.
		Practice at home	60 mins.
		Volunteer at shelter	60 mins.
		Walk dog	90 mins.
		Field hockey games	210 mins.
		Tutor sister in math	30 mins.
Total Time per Week:	1,200 mins.	*Total Time per Week:*	4,020 mins.

66 I'm a gymnast and I'm great on the balance beam. But I realized that I'm not so great when it comes to balancing fun and responsibilities. I had fun, but I had to squeeze fun in between all my responsibilities. I rushed from one thing to another, trying to get it all done. It was exhausting and overwhelming. After I learned a few skills to manage my stress, I started to feel less stressed and overwhelmed. Then I decided it was time to balance my life a little better. It wasn't easy. I had been out of balance for years. But I made some small changes, and it started to pay off. Now my life is less stressful and I'm enjoying the fun things I do more because I feel like I have time for them!

—Lois 99

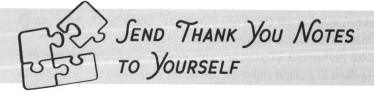

SEND THANK YOU NOTES TO YOURSELF

Over the years, you may have received thank you notes from people. They make you feel special and good, right? Although people say thank you to you all the time, there's something different about receiving a thank you note. Perhaps it's the time the person took to find the right card, to consider the right words, and to track down your address and mail it to you? Of course, it's more natural and comfortable to thank others than it is to thank yourself. Why thank yourself for just being you? Here's why: writing a thank you note to yourself reminds you of your strengths and the things that matter to you. Writing a thank you note to yourself highlights your passions and your dreams. Writing a thank you note to yourself invites you to pause, to reflect, to accept, and to appreciate who you are and where you've been and where you're going. To write thank you notes to yourself, follow these steps:

1. **Pick a place where you feel relaxed and comfortable and can write for at least 30 minutes without being interrupted.** Perhaps in your bedroom or in a hammock in the back yard. It doesn't matter as long as you're comfortable and you aren't likely to be interrupted.

2. **Decide whether you want to use a pen and paper or a computer.** If you decide to use pen and paper, write the notes in a small bound notebook. If you decide to use a computer, create a special document for the notes and add to the same document. In this way, you keep all your thank you notes in one place where you can re-read them sometimes when you want a little self-esteem boost.

3. **Choose your salutation and voice.** You may feel more comfortable starting with, "Dear Self," or you may want to use your name. You may want to write in first-person, "I want to thank you for . . ." or you may feel more comfortable writing in third-person, "Thank you, Alesandro, for your patience today."

4. **Set aside that critical inner voice and just write.** This might feel awkward at first, but remember that there's no right or wrong way to thank yourself. And no one has to see it but you! The important thing is that you're taking the time to do it.

5. **Try to be as specific as you can be.** Rather than writing, "You're a great friend," try "You're a kind and patient friend." You may want to quickly list things you're thanking yourself for rather than jumping into writing complete, grammatically correct sentences. A thank you note to yourself can include anything you wish to honor and celebrate about yourself. You can thank yourself for:
   - Challenges that you've overcome.
   - Good decisions that you've made.
   - Lessons that you've learned.
   - Risks that you've taken.
   - Things that you've accomplished.
   - Qualities that you like or admire about yourself (for example, that you're kind, loyal, positive, persistent, a good listener).

To get an idea of how to do this, look at Alesandro's thank you note to himself:

Dear Alesandro,

I wanted to thank you for being such a good friend to Jason today. I know Jason can be difficult. Sometimes he says mean things to you when he's upset with himself. You were very patient with him and showed that you're a kind and caring friend. Thank you for standing up for yourself too. That took guts to tell Jason how sometimes he says things to you that upset you. Jason apologized, like he always does, and you showed him how good a friend you are by accepting his apology. You've grown a lot over the last year. You're more confident about yourself, and your friendships are stronger than they've ever been. Most importantly, thank you for being you!

Sincerely yours,

Alesandro

> **"** This was REALLY hard. Thanking myself doesn't feel natural. I'm usually pretty hard on myself and thanking myself seems silly, especially for the little things that I accomplish, like a good grade on a pop quiz. But I noticed that when I thank myself for little accomplishments or for the little things that I like about myself, I feel better. It's just being a good friend to myself. Good friends say thank you for little things, not just big things, because little things count too.
> —Alesandro **"**

-🔆- *STRESS HACK:* If you don't have time to write a thank you note, take 15 seconds to just say thank you to yourself. For example, when you exercise Saturday morning rather sleeping in, say to yourself, "Thank you, Asif, for exercising today, your body is stronger now," or "Thank you, Kanesha, for not giving up on that tough history assignment." And when you thank yourself, smile a little. A little smile means that you accepted the thank you and the good feeling that comes with it.

-🔆- *STRESS HACK:* If you're crafty, create a gratitude box. Decorate a shoe or cigar box or coffee can, or even a paper bag. Then, every day, write down one thing you're grateful for and drop it in the gratitude box. It doesn't matter if you're grateful for the same thing every day, just write it down and drop it in. Whenever you're feeling down or less-than-grateful, open the box and read a note or two. It's an easy way to introduce a little perspective when you're feeling stressed or unhappy.

Touch Hand to Heart

Touch is a powerful experience. Touch not only soothes us but also enhances feelings of love, kindness, caring, and compassion. To create a quick moment of self-compassion, follow these steps:

1. Place one hand gently over your heart. Feel its warmth on your chest. Take a moment to acknowledge the simple act of giving a calm, comforting presence to yourself.

2. Breathe slowly, gently, and deeply into the space around your heart. Feel the warmth of your hand sink deeper and expand into your body.

3. Think of a specific time that you felt safe, loved, and cherished by another person: just one wonderful moment. The moment may be a memory of a time with a parent, grandparent, friend, therapist, teacher, or even pet.

4. As you remember this moment, let the warmth and good feelings wash through you. You might notice your muscles relaxing or a sigh escaping. A smile might come to the corners of your mouth. Just bathe in this warm feeling of acceptance and caring. Stay in this warm memory for 30 seconds.

5. When you're ready, bring your awareness back to the room or setting. Think about any shifts you felt in your body during this practice. Carry this sense of calm, ease, caring, and self-compassion into your day.

> **❝** The Touch Hand to Heart skill sounded pretty corny, so I decided to just hold one hand in the other, the way I remember my grandfather holding my hand when he walked me home from kindergarten. My grandfather was always there for me. No matter what I did or how I felt about myself, he always made me feel okay and like things would work out for me. Now, when I'm feeling a little stressed or down, I just put one hand in the other and remember Grandpa. I immediately feel less stressed and less alone.
> —Lois **❞**

-💡- *STRESS HACK:* Routines make life more predictable and therefore less stressful. However, when you're stuck in the same old routines, there's not much room for excitement, either. When you're stuck in routines, you're less likely to try new things. When you eat out, you might order the same thing. You might walk the same way to school each day. You might sit next to the same people and read the same kinds of books. Routines are comfortable, but when you're stuck in routines your life can start to feel stagnant, boring, and not a lot of fun. If you crave a little excitement, joy, and energy, try a new experience every day. They don't have to be big things. Changing the little things can add a bit of spice to your life. If you only watch horror shows, watch a rom com one night. If you only eat chocolate ice cream, try a scoop of strawberry. If you only wear earth-tone colors, wear something a little flashy. If you only sit with your friends at lunch, invite another person to join you. Even if you don't like any of these new experiences, you'll enjoy the excitement of trying something new.

-☼- *STRESS HACK:* An easy way to build more self-confidence is to recognize and spend time with the good in yourself. Pick one good thing that you like about yourself. For example, you might like that you're creative, or friendly, or athletic. Now, close your eyes and take a little time to take in this fact about yourself. But watch for signs that you're not taking it in. You might think: *What about the things I don't like about myself?* or *I'm not that way all the time.* Stand up to yourself and softly say, *It's okay that I'm not this way all the time. That's what it means to be human,* or *It's okay that I have things about me that I don't like. No human is perfect.* Open yourself to being convinced of it. Repeat this process several times each day and extend this to other good things about you.

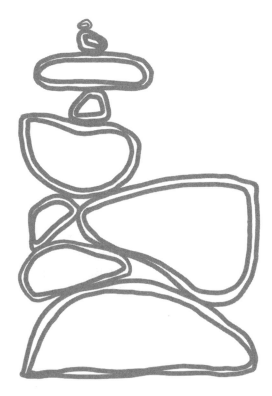

WRITE A LETTER OF RECOMMENDATION FOR YOURSELF

One day, people who are applying to schools or jobs might ask you to write letters of recommendation for them. A letter of recommendation highlights the positive strengths of the applicant while also describing their weaknesses in a fair and balanced way. Therefore, a good letter of recommendation balances praise and criticism. To build some positive self-esteem, try writing balanced letters of recommendation for yourself. Check out Deion's *Letter of Recommendation for Himself*. Would you hire him?

Dear Deion,

It's with great pleasure that I write a letter of recommendation for Deion. I've known Deion for 15 years and I've observed him in a variety of situations: at school, at home, on the soccer field, and with friends, teachers, and his family.

Determination is a word that I think of when I think Deion. He's great a lot of things: sports, guitar, puns, but math has always been hard for him. He has to worker harder than a lot of his friends to just pass math, but he's determined to do well. Math hasn't beaten Deion. He continues to try, although sometimes he puts off doing his math homework. I understand why. It's hard to get going sometimes but he always does.

Athletic is another word that describes Deion. He's great at any sport. He's strong, fast, and has a great mental game. Although Deion is great at sports, he doesn't always believe it. He can doubt his skills sometimes, especially before big games, this causes him to get really stressed out. But he's working with his coach on this and he's becoming more confident with every practice and game.

Loyal is another word that describes Deion. He's a loyal friend and if you're Deion's friend you know you can count on him when you're down or having a tough day. Deion always tries to apply the golden rule when it comes to his friends, "Do unto others as you would have them do unto you." His friends know this about Deion and respect him for it.

In conclusion, I highly recommend Deion. He's determined, a great athlete, and a good friend. He's a great guy and if you give him a chance you'll want to have him as a friend too.

Sincerely,

Deion

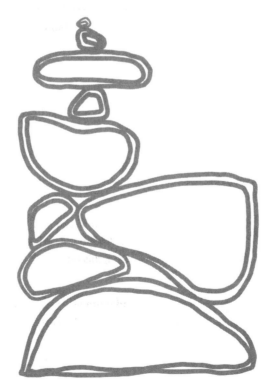

MEDITATE ON SELF-ACCEPTANCE

A sure-fire way to feel bad about yourself is to compare yourself to other people and focus on what you don't have that they do. You don't have Julie's blue eyes. You're not as smart as Simon. You're not as good a basketball player as Juan. Self-acceptance means that you're satisfied with everything about yourself—what you have and what you don't have. Self-acceptance means you accept yourself as the unique one-of-a-kind person that you are, regardless of your weaknesses or past mistakes. Self-acceptance can lower your stress and increase your happiness. Self-acceptance isn't easy, particularly when you're upset with yourself, but you can learn to accept yourself with practice. Meditating on self-acceptance is a great way to strengthen your self-acceptance muscle. Follow these steps to meditate on self-acceptance:

1. Make yourself comfortable. Once you're settled, close your eyes or soften your gaze and tune into your breath. Notice your breath, without trying to change it. And notice also if you feel tense or relaxed, without trying to change that either.

2. Inhale through your nose and then exhale through your mouth. Continue to take deep, full breaths in through your nose and out through your mouth. As you breathe, become aware of the state of your body and the quality of your mind. Where is your body holding tension? Do you feel closed off from your emotions? Where is your mind? Is it wandering or is it at home within the breath? Is your mind at ease or filled with restlessness, frustration, and doubt?

3. Place both hands over your heart and continue to inhale through your nose and exhale through your mouth. Ask yourself, "How does it feel to place my hands over this tender area, this place where I experience love for self and others?"

4. Let your breath become smoother and more effortless. Continue to breathe in and out through your nose. Feel the flow of air moving into your lungs and then out into the world.

5. With each exhale, imagine you are releasing any negative thoughts that may be lingering in your mind.

6. Continue to focus on your breath. On each inhale, think "I am okay," and on each exhale, think "I am enough." Let each inhale draw in self-acceptance and each exhale release what is no longer helpful to you. Take a few minutes to breathe and recite "I am okay" and "I am enough" internally. Notice how you feel as you say these words to yourself.

7. If your mind wanders at any point, know that it's okay. It's the nature of the mind to wander. Simply bring your attention back to the breath. Notice how your thoughts come and go, whether positive or negative, and simply allow them to pass by like clouds floating in the sky.

8. Now visualize yourself standing in front of a mirror, and look into your own eyes. What do you see? Hurt and anger? Guilt and sadness? Love and joy? Neutral feelings?

9. Regardless of what appears in the reflection, tell yourself, "I love you," "You are beautiful," and "You are worthy of happiness." Know that what you see in the mirror in this moment may be different from what you see the next time you look.

10. Imagine now that you could breathe into your heart and visualize love pouring out of your hands and into your heart.

11. Let this love warm you and expand from your heart center, filling the rest of your body.

12. Feel a sense of comfort and calm traveling up through your chest into your neck and head, out into your shoulders, arms, and hands, and then down into your ribs, belly, pelvis, legs, and feet.

13. Allow a sensation of warmth to fill you from head to toe. Breathe into that place and know that acceptance is always available for you when you need it.

14. When you're ready, take a few more deep, mindful breaths and then gently open your eyes. Sit for a few moments to acknowledge the unique experience you had during this meditation. This is a beautiful opportunity to learn something new about yourself and tune into your physical and emotional needs. Let self-acceptance enable you to build a stronger relationship with yourself and allow you to show up more fully in your life.

66 When I first read about self-acceptance, I didn't even know what that meant. I always thought that I had to push myself to be a better student, a better athlete, a better friend, and a better son. I put a lot of pressure on myself, and it was kind of scary to think about just accepting myself for how I am now. I thought that meant giving up on trying to achieve things, that I'd lose everything I've worked so hard to get, or that I'd lose the motivation to work hard. But I decided to try a little self-acceptance. I started meditating on self-acceptance and the only thing that changed was that I felt better about myself. I still had the motivation, but I wasn't so hard on myself when I missed shot or got a C on a quiz. Self-acceptance actually makes it easier to celebrate my successes because it feels like I deserve them.

—Asif **99**

Spend Time with Your Best Self

Some people who tend to feel very stressed don't like themselves all that much. They wouldn't take themselves to the prom. They wouldn't invite themselves to lunch. They wouldn't ask themselves to run for class president. However, you can learn to like yourself in the same way that you can learn to like skateboarding, or painting in watercolors, or baking bread. It just takes practice and an openness to the possibility that you're worth liking both on the surface and deep down.

One way to learn to like yourself is to spend more time with the good stuff about you. You can spend time with the self who made the final goal that won the soccer game. You can spend time with the self who got a B on the super tough math quiz. Not only does spending time with good stuff about you boost your self-esteem, it also creates pleasant feelings that combat stress, worry, and sadness. To spend time with your best self, follow these steps:

1. On a blank sheet of paper, list six good things you like about yourself (maybe you have great balance on a skateboard) or things people compliment you about (you might have great fashion sense) or successes that you have had (a good grade on a pop quiz).

2. For each of the good things about yourself on the list:
   • Describe where you were and what was happening
   • Describe the good feelings that you felt (happy, proud, satisfied, etc.).
   • Describe what you were thinking when you were feeling good about yourself.
   • Describe your role in making this good thing happen (for example, "I talked to Jay to remind him to pass to me a little more.")

3. Close your eyes and replay in your mind the story about your best self. Savor the feelings and open yourself to liking the person you are.

STRESS HACK: You've likely heard that it takes more muscles to frown than it takes to smile, but even a small smile at the end of a long stressful day, or a tiny smile during a difficult moment, can feel nearly impossible to muster. But as difficult as it feels to smile sometimes, you'll actually feel better when you do. You usually smile when you feel happy. It seems kind of backwards to smile *to* feel happy, but it works. Smiling tricks your brain into releasing chemicals that create happy feelings. Even a half smile can trick your brain into a moment of happiness. Not only that, but when you smile, people around you smile back and you'll feel even better.

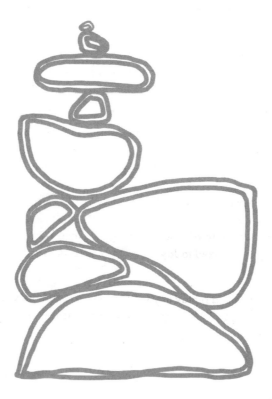

Focusing on kindness and goodwill toward others can help you feel better about yourself. When practiced daily for 15 minutes, this loving kindness meditation can lift your spirits, boost your mood, and alleviate the anxiety and stress that built over the day. You may wish to read the following script aloud into a recording device. You can then listen to the recording with your eyes closed:

Become comfortable in your chair or bed, and sit upright with your shoulders relaxed. [Pause 5 seconds]. Allow your hands to rest comfortably in your lap. Gently close your eyes [Pause 10 seconds]. Settle into awareness of the body and the breath.

Feel into your body right now . . . notice what's there. Be open to whatever is to be experienced in the body in this moment. Connect to the breath. Notice the wave-like movements of the belly [Pause 10 seconds].

Now, allow yourself to remember and open up to your basic goodness. You might remember times when you've been kind or generous. You might recall your natural desire to be happy and not to suffer. If acknowledging your own goodness is difficult, look at yourself through the eyes of someone who loves you. What does that person love about you? Or recall the unconditional love you felt from a cherished pet [Pause 20 seconds].

If it allows tender feelings of kindness to flow more easily, imagine yourself as a young child, standing before you. Perhaps when you were four or five years old. As you experience this love, notice how you feel in your body. Maybe you feel warmth in the face. Perhaps you notice a smile on your face or a sense of expansiveness. This is lovingkindness, a natural feeling that is accessible to all of us, always. Rest with this feeling of open, unconditional love for a few moments [Pause 20 seconds]. Let yourself bask in the energy of lovingkindness. Breathe it in and breathe it out as you invite feelings of peace and acceptance [Pause 20 seconds].

Begin now to wish yourself well by extending words of lovingkindness to yourself. Use the phrases offered here or alter these phrases and choose whatever words express your wishes of loving kindness toward yourself and others. And now, offering these words in your mind for yourself:

- May I be filled with lovingkindness.
- May I be held in lovingkindness.
- May I feel connected and calm.
- May I accept myself just as I am.
- May I be happy.
- May I know the natural joy of being alive.

Now open the circle of lovingkindness by bringing to mind someone who is dear to you. Someone you care about and who has always been supportive. Reflect on this person's basic goodness, sensing what it is in particular that you love about them. In your heart feel your appreciation for this dear one, and begin your simple offering:

- May you be filled with lovingkindness.
- May you be held in lovingkindness.
- May you feel my love now.
- May you accept yourself just as you are.
- May you be happy.
- May you know the natural joy of being alive.

Now bring to mind a "neutral" person. This is someone you might see regularly but don't know well. It might be a neighbor, or a grocery store clerk. Bring this person to mind now, and repeat the words of loving kindness:

- May you be filled with lovingkindness.
- May you be held in lovingkindness.
- May you feel my love now.
- May you accept yourself just as you are.
- May you be happy.
- May you know the natural joy of being alive.

And now, if it's possible for you, bring to mind someone with whom you've had a difficult relationship. Perhaps it's someone you don't like and for whom it's difficult for you to feel sympathy or compassion. See if it's possible to let go of feelings of resentment and dislike for this person. Remind yourself to see this person as a whole being, deserving of love and kindness, and as someone who feels pain, stress, and anxiety, as someone who also suffers. See if it's possible to extend to this person the words of lovingkindness in your mind:

- May you be filled with lovingkindness.
- May you be held in lovingkindness.
- May you feel my love now.
- May you accept yourself just as you are.
- May you be happy.
- May you know the natural joy of being alive.

Now, allow your awareness to open out in all directions: yourself, a dear one, a neutral person, and a difficult person. Open to all beings, humans, and animals living everywhere. Living in richness, poverty, war, peace, hunger, abundance. Aware of all the joys and sorrows that all beings experience:

- May all beings be filled with lovingkindness.
- May all beings be held in lovingkindness.
- May all beings feel my love now.
- May all beings accept themselves just as they are.
- May all beings be happy.
- May all beings know the natural joy of being alive.

And now, bring this practice to a close by coming back to extend kindness to yourself. Sit for a while and bask in the energy of loving kindness that may have been generated here.

-⚙️- *STRESS HACK:* For some people, it doesn't feel natural to be kind to themselves. If that's you, a good place to start is to treat yourself the way you would treat others that you care about. If a friend is feeling down, hurt, or upset, you might pat them on the back or hold their hand. You might say something kind or soothing to them, such as, "That's really hard," or "You're okay just the way you are." Next time you're upset with yourself, close your eyes, hold one hand in the other, rest a hand on your shoulder, or wrap your arms around yourself for a hug, and say softly to yourself, "You're okay just the way you are."

💡 *STRESS HACK:* Have you noticed that you feel a bit happier and more upbeat on sunny days than overcast days? It's the same with people. When you're surrounded by positive people, their positive outlook is contagious. You feel more positive. You can't help it. However, you can't always decide who is around you. Sometimes the person is positive and sometimes the person is negative. But you can gradually limit contact with people who bring you down every time you speak with them. If the relationship is important, you don't have to cut off all contact with the person. Just try to limit the kinds of conversations you have and the time you spend hanging out with the person. For example, if you're feeling a little bummed about the relationship with your significant other, you might not want to share this with someone who tends to go negative about relationships. Just focus on small talk and save this conversation for a friend who is more positive and optimistic, or at least not overly negative.

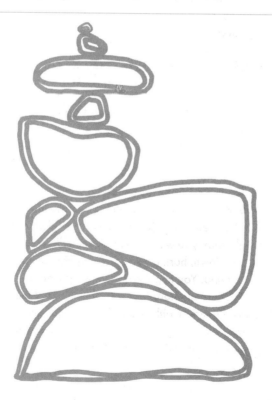

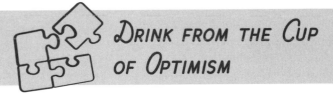

Drink from the Cup of Optimism

The attitude people take toward events in life affects how they feel about them. To feel less stressed by events, try drinking from the cup of optimism instead of pessimism. In other words, reframe your attitude. For example, when you think about the test tomorrow, do you think, "I'm totally going to bomb the test"? or do you think, "I'll probably do better than I think I will. I usually do"? Or, when a friend invites you to a party, do you think, "I'm not going to enjoy myself," or do you think, "I'll probably enjoy myself at least some, and I'll certainly have more fun than sitting at home thinking about the fun my friend is having"?

We all have a pessimistic attitude sometimes, but this attitude isn't always accurate or true. You can learn to reframe your pessimistic attitudes into optimistic attitudes, or at least into more realistic attitudes. Here are examples of reframing pessimistic attitudes into optimistic attitudes. Give it a try. Follow these steps to drink from the cup of optimism:

1. On a blank sheet of paper, draw two vertical lines to make three columns. At the top of the left column, write **Pessimistic Attitude**. At the top of the middle column, write **Optimistic Attitude**. At the top of the right column, write **Facts**.

2. Now, think of a situation or event about which you're feeling stressed or pessimistic and write the situation at the top of the page.

3. In the **Pessimistic Attitude** column, write the negative or pessimistic thoughts you're having about the situation that make you feel especially stressed or upset.

4. In the **Optimistic Attitude** column, write more realistic, positive, or optimistic thoughts that could help you feel good rather than stressed or upset.

5. Last, in the **Facts** column, write what really happened at the event or in the situation. Only the facts, and not your interpretation of them!

Ofelia decided to *Drink from the Cup of Optimism* about two events: an argument she had with her boyfriend, and about running for class president. Look at her *Drink from the Cup of Optimism Exercise* to see how she did it.

OFELIA'S DRINK FROM THE CUP
OF OPTIMISM EXERCISE

Event

Tim and I argued about how much time he spends gaming with his friends rather than seeing me.

Pessimistic Attitude	Optimistic Attitude	Facts
He doesn't love me. If he did, he'd spend his free time with me.	Tim tells me that he loves me. It's not realistic to expect him to spend all his free time with me. I don't spend every free minute I have with him.	Tim texted me several times while he was gaming with his friends. He said he wanted to see me later and we did.

Event

I'm running for class president and the election is today.

Pessimistic Attitude	Optimistic Attitude	Facts
There's no way I'll win.	My friends say that it'll be a close race but my chances are as good as anyone else running.	It was a close race and I won!

-💡- *STRESS HACK:* Hanging around optimistic people can help you see the glass as half full rather than half empty. If your friends have a pessimistic attitude toward life, you'll tend to see things from their point of view. It's not necessary to dump your pessimistic friends, just add optimistic friends to balance out the doom and gloom. Also, if a friend starts to go negative, smile and change the subject, or offer a glass half full take on things. Who knows, you just might help a friend feel a little better.

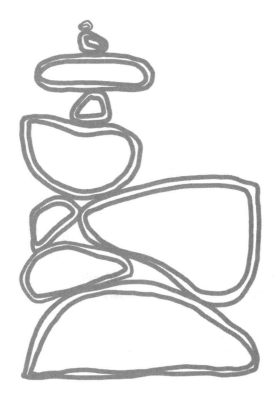

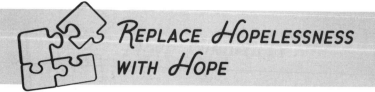

REPLACE HOPELESSNESS WITH HOPE

When you feel stressed or down, you might view the future as bleak and hopeless. You can learn to replace hopelessness with hope, and a hope box is a fun and easy way to do that. A hope box is a box you fill with items that help you feel inspired, optimistic, and hopeful about the future. You can fill your hope box with anything: pictures, poetry, letters, prayer cards, bible verses, even mementos like a beautiful stone or pressed flower that reminds you of better times. To create and use a hope box, follow these steps:

1. Think of items that you want to place in your hope box. The items can be anything that fits in the box, as long as the item inspires hope, optimism, and good feelings. You might ask a trusted friend or family member for ideas. Here are a few ideas to get you started:

HOPE KIT ITEMS

Short inspirational newspaper or magazine articles	Programs from fun concerts or sporting events you've attended	A list of events (your prom, graduation, wedding) that you're looking forward to
Reminders to listen to inspirational songs	Soothing items like hand lotion, yarn, or cloth to rub	Soothing fragrances like scented candles or lotions
Special items from nature	Inspirational poems or quotes	Pictures from magazines
Award ribbons or medals that you've received	Baby photos of you or of a loved one	Photos of friends and special family members
A favorite scarf or small item of clothing that you like	Small gifts from friends or family members	Comforting or inspiring letters from friends or family
Birthday or graduation cards people sent you	Caring letters you wrote yourself	Letters of recommendation you wrote for yourself

2. Decorate the box and place the items in it. You can always add more items later, too. Tell a trusted friend or family member about your hope box. During difficult times, they can remind you to go through the hope box or, better yet, go through the hope box with you.

3. Now that you've made your hope box, here's how to use it. Several times during the day go through it. Pick up each item and connect with the hopeful feelings it generates for you. If it's a poem or an article, read it aloud to yourself. If it's a special stone or award, hold the item and remember where you were when you found it or who gave it to you, and what you were doing and feeling. If it's a list of special songs, listen to the songs and sing along.

> ❝ I told Ms. Hermosa, my art teacher, about my hope box. She loved the idea. She's my favorite teacher. I always go to her when I'm having a tough day. We talked about how I could decorate the box, and I decided to decorate it the way Frida Kahlo would decorate it. I painted the box and pasted interesting photos of flowers from magazines I liked, and added some glitter and small plastic coins and animals I found in the art closet. Over the next few weeks, I filled it with interesting things. As I added new things, I told Ms. Hermosa why they were special to me. That felt really good. Ms. Hermosa even gave me a few things that were special to her, like a photo of her new puppy, and a ribbon she wore in her hair. Now, when I'm feeling stressed or down, I go through the box and feel better. Life doesn't seem so hard when I spend a little time with hope.
>
> —Lois ❞

Give Back

To give back means to help others. There are many benefits of giving back. When you give back, you lower your stress, boost your mood, and increase your well-being. When you give back, you feel better about yourself. When you give back, you gain perspective on your life and the lives of others, which can help you enjoy each moment and each thing in your life. Giving back reminds you that other people struggle too, which helps you feel less alone with your own struggles. Last, giving back provides deeper meaning and purpose to your life. In a sense, giving back is its own reward.

Now that you've learned skills to manage stress, you likely have more time and energy to give to others or to causes that are important to you. Giving back starts with thinking about the skills and talents you have that you can use to give back. Then, you match your skills and talents to one or two opportunities in your community.

SKILLS, TALENTS, AND OPPORTUNITIES TO GIVE BACK

Skills and Talents

Draw	Make jewelry	Work on cars
Dance	Play chess	Paint
Bake	Do math	Ride a bike
Knit or crochet	Play a sport	Garden
Woodwork	Write poetry or stories	Take photographs
Swim	Draw	Program computers
Do crafts	Type	Bake or cook
Sing, whistle, yodel	Scrapbook	Play an instrument
Skateboard	Surf	Make model airplanes
Play cards or checkers	Do crossword puzzles	Sail

Opportunities

Tutor kids	Clean up a local park	Donate food
Mow lawns or garden	Paint houses	Coach sports
Organize bake sales	Assist teachers	Write to people in prison
Make phone calls	Teach English	Babysit
Donate blood	Make lunches for people who are homeless	Visit a senior center
Write military personnel	Answer phones for crisis line	Fundraise for good cause
Foster animals	Recycle for community	Volunteer at animal shelter
Organize block party	Volunteer at legal aid office	Participate in walk-a-thons

-☼- *STRESS HACK:* A fun way to give back is through small, random acts of kindness. Each day, try to do something kind. Small things are fine. In fact, small acts of kindness are great, because they're easier to do and therefore you'll do them more often. Drop some change into the guitar case of the street musician. Buy an extra donut and give one to someone who's hungry. Write poems or draw a picture and leave these on park benches. Smile and say hello to people you pass on the sidewalk. Compliment a neighbor's garden. Pick flowers from your garden and place them on the tables in cafes you visit. Put out bird seed to attract birds to your neighborhood. These small acts of random kindness benefit others, but they're really for you.

🌰 In a Nutshell

Life isn't just about managing stress; it's about thriving, too. Thriving means feeling good about yourself and your life, and feeling confident that you have the skills not only to manage stress, but to build a life that is rewarding and fulfilling. All the skills you've learned, if practiced regularly, can create and maintain a life that is less stressful, more positive, and worth living deeply and passionately.

STRESS SKILL QUICK LOCATER

Skill	Inside or Outside Skill	Page Number
School and Work Stress		
Breathe Slowly and Deeply	Inside	38
Relax Your Body	Inside	40
Relax and Refresh	Inside	42
Identify Your Thinking Traps	Inside	44
Catch It, Check It, and Change It	Inside	48
Divide and Conquer	Outside	53
Schedule Time	Outside	56
Estimate Time Accurately	Outside	58
Do It Now	Outside	61
Make Good Decisions Quickly	Outside	66
Performance and Test Stress		
Recover from Mistakes	Inside	70
Focus to Finish	Inside	75
Imagine Success	Inside	79
Slip into the Present Moment	Inside	86
Move Mindfully	Inside	89
Reset Your Predict-o-meter	Inside	91
Calculate Your Prediction Accuracy	Inside	94
Surf the Panic Wave	Inside	97
Coach Yourself to a Win	Inside	105
Build Routines	Outside	110
Family and Friend Stress		
Communicate Calmly and Clearly	Outside	116
Walk Down the Conflict Staircase	Outside	119
Think It Through to the End	Inside	121

Skill	Inside or Outside Skill	Page Number
Do One Thing at a Time	Outside	198
Overcome Fear of Missing Out	Inside	202
Tell Your Side of the Story	Outside	205
Handle Cyberbullying	Outside	207
Deal with Boredom Off-Device	Inside	210
Health and Hormone Stress		
Build a Consistent Sleep Schedule	Outside	216
Build a Sleep Wind-Down Routine	Outside	218
Deal with Unfinished Business	Inside	221
Savor to Sleep Better	Inside	225
Tell Your Body to Relax	Inside	227
Build an Out-of-Bed-in-the-Morning Plan	Outside	228
Build a Stay-Alert Plan	Outside	230
Try Yoga Instead of Yawns	Outside	232
Exercise Your Way to a Calmer Self	Outside	234
Eat Your Way to a Calmer Self	Outside	237
Thriving		
Keep Your Balance	Inside	240
Send Thank You Notes to Yourself	Inside	245
Touch Hand to Heart	Inside	248
Write a Letter of Recommendation for Yourself	Inside	251
Meditate on Self-Acceptance	Inside	253
Spend Time with Your Best Self	Inside	256
Meditate on Loving Kindness	Inside	258
Drink from the Cup of Optimism	Inside	262
Replace Hopelessness with Hope	Inside	265
Give Back	Outside	267

 RESOURCES

Readings for Teens

Hansen, S. A. (2013). *The executive functioning workbook for teens: Help for unprepared, late and scattered teens*. New Harbinger Publications.

Honos-Webb, L. (2011). *The ADHD workbook for teens*. New Harbinger Publications.

Knauss, W. (2016). *Overcoming procrastination for teens: A CBT guide for college-bound students*. New Harbinger Publications.

Quinn, P. O., & Maitland, T. E. L. (2011). *On your own: A college readiness guide for teens with ADHD/LD*. Magination Press.

Sisemore, T. A. (2010). *Free from OCD: A workbook for teens with obsessive-compulsive disorder*. New Harbinger Publications.

Skeen, M., McKay, M., Fanning, P., & Skeen, K. (2016). *Communication skills for teens*. New Harbinger Publications.

Tompkins, M. A. (2022). *The anxiety and depression workbook for teens: Simple CBT skills to help you deal with anxiety, worry, and sadness*. New Harbinger Publications.

Tompkins, M. A. (2020). *Zero to 60: A teen's guide to manage frustration, anger, and everyday irritations*. Magination Press.

Tompkins, M. A., & Barkin, J. R. (2018). *The relaxation and stress reduction workbook for teens: CBT skills to help you deal with worry and anxiety*. New Harbinger Publications.

Tompkins, M. A., & Martinez, K. (2009). *My anxious mind: A teen's guide to managing anxiety and panic*. Magination Press.

Tompkins, M. A., & Thompson, M. Q. (2018). *The insomnia workbook for teens: Skills to help you stop stressing and start sleeping better*. New Harbinger Publications.

Toner, J. B., & Freeland, C. A. B. (2016). *Depression: A teen's guide to survive and thrive*. Magination Press.

Zucker, B. (2022). *A perfectionist's guide to not being perfect*. Magination Press.

Readings for Parents

Anxiety

Achar Josephs, S. (2017). *Helping your anxious teen: Positive parenting strategies to help your teen beat anxiety, stress, and worry.* New Harbinger Publications.

Chansky, T. E. (2014). *Freeing your child from anxiety: Practical strategies to overcome fears, worries, and phobias and be prepared for life—From toddlers to teens.* Harmony.

Attention-Deficit-Hyperactivity Disorder

Barkley, R. A. (2013). *Taking charge of ADHD: The complete authoritative guide for parents* (3rd ed.). Guilford Press.

Guare, R., & Dawson, P. (2012). *Smart but scattered teens: The "executive skills" program for helping teens reach their potential.* Guilford Press.

Depression

Mondimore, F. M., & Kelly, P. (2015). *Adolescent depression: A guide for parents.* John Hopkins University Press.

Medication

Wilens, T. E., & Hammerness, P. G. (2016). *Straight talk about psychiatric medications for kids* (4th ed.). Guilford Press.

Online Resources

Cognitive Behavioral Therapy

The following associations provide teens and parents with qualified mental health professionals who specialize in cognitive behavioral therapy for a variety of problems, such as anxiety, anger, and depression:

Academy of Cognitive Therapy
academyofct.org

Anxiety and Depression Association of America
adaa.org

Association for Behavioral and Cognitive Therapies
abct.org

Beck Institute for Cognitive Behavior Therapy
beckinstitute.org

International OCD Foundation
iocdf.org

Professional Associations

The following professional associations provide teens and parents with brochures, tips, and articles on the psychological and emotional issues that affect a person's physical and emotional well-being:

American Academy of Child and Adolescent Psychiatry
aacap.org

American Psychiatric Association
psych.org

American Psychological Association
apa.org

Sleep

The following websites provide information to professionals and the public on sleep disorders, sleep hygiene, sleep treatments and accredited sleep laboratories and centers in their area:

American Academy of Sleep Medicine
aasmnet.org

American Insomnia Association
americaninsomniaassociation.org

National Sleep Foundation (NSF)
sleepfoundation.org

Bullying

The following websites provide information and videos to professionals and the public on bullying and resources and strategies to intervene to assist teens who are bullied:

PACER's National Bullying Prevention Center
pacer.org/bullying

Stop Bullying Now.
splcenter.org

PREVNet
prevnet.ca

Bullying Prevention Program
bullyfree.com/

WITS
witsprogram.ca/

They do a curriculum based on the movie, "Finding Kind":
youtube.com/watch?v=NgzdcGE-3Gc

Kind Campaign
kindcampaign.com/

Trauma

The following websites provide information to professionals and the public on trauma and childhood abuse:

American Professional Society on the Abuse of Children apsac.org
CARES Institute caresinstitute.org
Center for Traumatic Stress in Children and Adolescents
Allegheny General Hospital pittsburghchildtrauma.org
International Society for Traumatic Stress Studies istss.org
National Child Traumatic Stress Network nctsnet.org
National Crime Victims Research and Treatment Center https://medicine.musc.edu/departments/psychiatry/divisions-and-programs/divisions/ncvc
Medical University of South Carolina musc.edu/cvc

Health information

The following U.S. government websites provide information on physical and mental health:

Food and Drug Administration (FDA)
fda.gov

National Institute of Health (NIH)
nih.gov

National Institute of Mental Health (NIMH)
nimh.nih.gov

Mobile Apps

Breath2Relax
Learn and practice diaphragmatic breathing and detailed information on the effects of stress on the body.

Happify
Learn and practice activities that can help you combat negativity, anxiety, and stress while fostering positive traits like gratitude and empathy.

Headspace
Learn and practice a series of guided meditations and mindfulness exercises.

My Mood Tracker
Helps you track your mood. As you become more aware of what you're feeling when, you can begin to figure out links between life events and cycles and your moods, which in turn will help you manage (and work around) your moods.

Pay It Forward
Learn and practice a daily act of kindness—a proven stress reducer—with a list of suggestions as well as connection to a community of people who are committed to the principles of paying it forward.

The Mindfulness App
Learn and practice five guided meditations, with options for listening to calming music or nature sounds.

INDEX

CKNOWLEDGMENTS

When I take on any challenge, I guarantee that I'll feel at least some stress along the way. Writing this book was no exception. I would like to acknowledge the people who helped me move through the stress, the doubt, and (truth be told) the procrastination I experienced in writing this book. First, I thank my colleagues (Emily Berner, Joan Davidson, Daniela Owen, and Monique Thompson) at the San Francisco Bay Area Center for Cognitive Therapy. They are the calming and supportive harbor that is my professional home. Also, I want to extend special thanks to Judy Beck and Jackie Persons. It's difficult to put into words the impact these thoughtful, kind, and supersmart clinicians and friends have had on my professional and personal life.

I thank Kristine Enderle, editorial director of Magination Press, for her steady support of this book and for her unimaginable patience with my writing process. This is the third book I've written with Kristine at the helm. I can say without reservation, she's a wonderful guide through the uncharted and sometimes choppy waters of writing a book. I also thank Katie Ten Hagen, editor at Magination Press, for her thorough and thoughtful editing. She greatly improved the quality of the book that you have in your hands.

I thank my life partner, Luann DeVoss, for her unwavering support of this project. This book is my fifteenth and therefore her fifteenth. She never complained: not once. Remarkable! I thank my daughters, Madeleine and Olivia, who are awesome young women in every way. I am honored to be their dad.

Last, I thank the many teens and their parents who have come to me for help over the years. I thought of you often as I worked on the book and realized that I learned as much if not more from you about managing stress than you learned from me. We are a great team! Thanks to you all.

About the Author

Michael A. Tompkins, PhD, ABPP, is a licensed psychologist and board certified in behavioral and cognitive psychology by the American Board of Professional Psychology. He is the co-director of the San Francisco Bay Area Center for Cognitive Therapy, a faculty member for the Beck Institute for Cognitive Behavior Therapy, and for the International OCD Foundation Training Institute. He is the author of fifteen books, including two others published by Magination Press: *My Anxious Mind: A Teen's Guide to Managing Anxiety and Panic* (2010), *Zero to 60: A Teen's Guide to Manage Frustration, Anger, and Everyday Irritations* (2020), and *The Anxiety and Depression Workbook for Teens: Simple CBT Skills to Help You Deal with Anxiety, Worry, and Sadness* (2022). Dr. Tompkins serves on the advisory board of Magination Press, the children's imprint of the American Psychological Association.

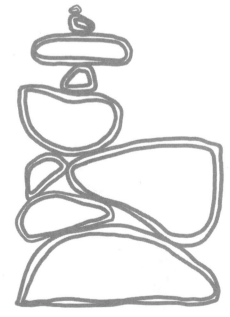

Keep Reading! More Books to Help You Be Your Best

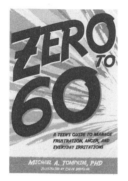

ZERO TO 60

A TEEN'S GUIDE TO MANAGE FRUSTRATION, ANGER, AND EVERYDAY IRRITATIONS

BY MICHAEL A. TOMPKIN, PhD

FIND YOUR FIERCE

HOW TO PUT SOCIAL ANXIETY IN ITS PLACE

BY JACQUELINE SPERLING, PhD

ILLUSTRATED BY ANYA KUVARZINA

A Perfectionist's Guide to NOT Being Perfect

by Bonnie Zucker

DEPRESSION A TEEN'S GUIDE TO SURVIVE AND THRIVE

BY JACQUELINE B. TONER, PhD AND CLAIRE A.B. FREELAND, PhD

MY ANXIOUS MIND: A TEEN'S GUIDE TO MANAGING ANXIETY AND PANIC

by Michael A. Tompkin, PhD & Katherine Martinez, PhD

Illustrated by Michael Sloan

LIKE ABILITY

THE TRUTH ABOUT POPULARITY

BY LORI GETZ, MA & MITCH PRINSTEIN, PhD

GIRL

Love, Sex, Romance and Being You

by Karen Rayne, PhD

TRANS+

LOVE, SEX, ROMANCE, AND BEING YOU

BY KATHRYN GONZALES, MBA AND KAREN RAYNE, PhD

ALL THE FEELINGS UNDER THE SUN

HOW TO DEAL WITH CLIMATE CHANGE

by Leslie Davenport, illustrated by Jessica Smith

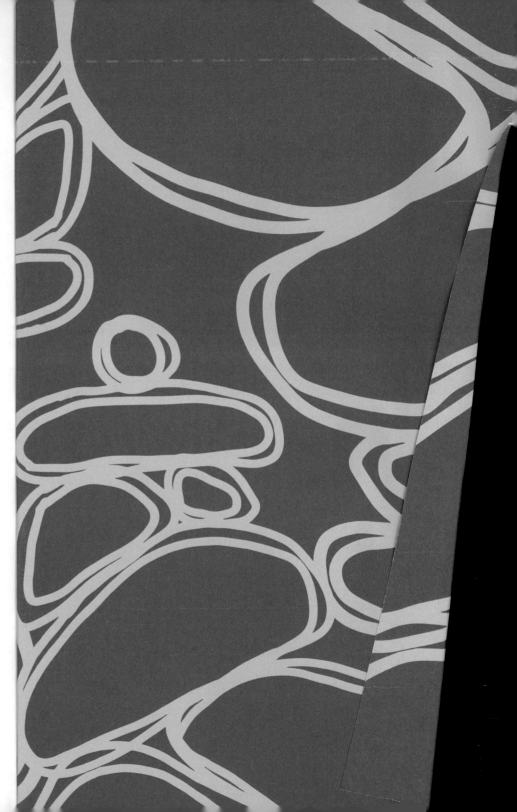